POWER THINKING

How to develop the potential of the
mind and generate creative and effective
thinking.

POWER THINKING

How to Develop the Energy Potential of Your Mind

by
E. H. SHATTOCK

TURNSTONE PRESS LIMITED
Wellingborough, Northamptonshire

First published 1983
Second Impression 1984

British Library Cataloguing in Publication Data

Shattock, E.H.
    Power Thinking.
    1. Self-actualization (Psychology)
    I. Title
    158'.1   BF637.S4
    ISBN 0-85500-192-5

*Turnstone Press is part of the
Thorsons Publishing Group*

Printed and bound in Great Britain

CONTENTS

INTRODUCTION

The description of the tools of the mind in this book is based on the experience, knowledge, and conviction, that mind and brain are separate organs of the human body, the functioning of which are linked. The brain is dependent on mind for the directions it gives for all the activities of the physical body. The brain is purely a physical organ; mind an instrument controlling mental matter. All that follows in this book makes sense only on the concept of two separately operating connected organs which together handle the process of thought and action. I know that there are many persons, including responsible and well-known scientists, who will not accept such a proposition. To them, thought is simply the result of chemical changes in the brain. There is no such thing as a mind working in mental matter; all is prescribed within the physical limits of the brain. Because this is probably a widely held concept by those who trouble to think about such matters, the suggestion that mind and brain are separate and complementary organs should be regarded only as a hypothesis by all who read this book, unless they already have experience leading to conviction that mind is the director of energy, via the brain, to the human being's physical vehicle of expression.

The tools, some of which are less well understood than others, are ways of procuring the conditions which the mind requires in order to give of its best, and the actual methods or techniques to be employed to empower thought with its maximum available energy. 'Tool' is, therefore, a word used to describe a particular physical and mental condition, or a detail of technique that can be isolated, understood, and then consciously applied.

These tools, I would emphasize, apply to the transfer of thought to the brain and to its result in the physical body. The body has many means of interfering with the process of thought, and the tools I have called 'setting-up tools' are designed to offset these. The 'action tools' are the methods of using the mind so as to attract the maximum amount of energy to thought. This is where we, at present, so lamentably fail. The mind, that most intricate of instruments must, in the same way that we treat a sophisticated machine, first be set up, and then given the right tool for the job in hand. These have to be selected. Not all the tools are required for many mental actions. One has to select what is needed for the particular kind of mental activity one is pursuing, just as an engineer on a repair job takes from his tool kit the special tools that he will want for it. What these tools do is to maximise the power of the mind, that is, to increase the amount of energy that the thoughts will carry.

In considering the working of mind in relation to the physical body, we come up against two elements in the line of communication that appear to be working in entirely different media — the mind and the brain. We do not yet know how the connection is made between them. The mind has the task of working through what is usually a very imperfect body, so that it is a wonder that it works as efficiently as it does. I hope many will find that, by adopting the techniques described in this book, the mind will be able to carry greater energy to its task, whether it is consciously or subconsciously directed. Such a small proportion of the mind-power that could be made available is actually brought to bear on our common daily activities, that we can have no idea of the effect of the employment of its full potential.

In the greater part of this book I am considering mind only in relation to the physical body, not as it can, should, and will be used to initiate those expansions of consciousness that will increase our awareness of the reality behind physical form, and of our relationship to those higher beings in whose hands the spiritual development of mankind is entrusted. That is the subject of esoteric teaching for which many schools and groups exist at the present time, of which the most widely known in the western world is probably the Arcane School, with its headquarters in New York, London, Geneva, and Tokyo. This school comprises thousands of students enrolled from all the countries of the world. It teaches, first, a vertical extension of the mind's field of activity, and only when that has begun to influence the personality of a student, shows how to make use of this to extend the horizontal reach of the mind. In this book I am only concerned with the horizontal extension in the world of phenomena, and the way to increase this by giving this wonderful instrument the right environment and developing the right techniques to enable it to display its proper force and energy.

These two developments, vertical and horizontal, complement each other; they cannot truly be separated; there is always a degree of each in the mind's activity. The purification of mind, of its motives and of its total activity, must have progressed to a point where it has left the field of personality objectives behind, before the mind can be entrusted with the formidable power that lies latent within it. It can, however, be developed and used purely for selfish motives, to increase the power of the personality and to ride roughshod over one's fellow human beings when they stand in the way. Many have achieved these powers in varying degrees, as we well know, and in the example of Hitler, we have a man well endowed with this kind of power which he used to evil ends. To do this requires very strong determination and mental power above the average. It is fortunate that the obstacles in the way of power without purification are such as to prevent all but the very few successfully embarking on what is called 'the left hand path'.

In order to release this latent power of the mind, we need to follow a programme of self-discipline leading to the gradual overcoming of the pull of the personality. This can only be achieved by a life of study and meditation. Study in order to learn what these powers are, how they originate, and how to put them into practice for the good of mankind, and meditation in order to clear away the obstructions between the mind and the one essence that lies behind it. This essence awaits the blossoming of contact between the personality and itself, before it can take over direction of all the personality's activities. These parallel lines of purpose, study and meditation, will inevitably lead to an individual being gradually permitted to use his growing power, because it will be used only for the benefit of mankind. The programme of expanding mental power is one of which we ought to be aware, so that we can make the choice either to follow it or not. However, this is not what we shall be considering in the chapters that follow, what we are going to look at is how to prepare the background to mental action so that we can derive the maximum power that is available from our mind *in its present state of development*.

There is, of course, the problem of just how the mind, in manipulating mental matter, is able to affect the brain; this is rather loosely referred to as 'mind over matter'. Somewhere there is a connecting link that enables the mental energy we generate to initiate physical action. This problem would appear to be insoluble to one who does not accept the reality of the 'etheric body', the energy body lying behind each cell and organ of the physical body and controlling all its activities. This body, which can be seen by those people who have clairvoyant or psychic vision — and there are a great many more such people than one would expect — is formed of streams of fine matter in motion, which is another way of describing energy. The energy feeds every part of the physical body with what is required for its maintenance and health, and it is according to whether the supply is adequate, in excess, or deficient, that the state of bodily health is determined.

It is on this etheric body that mind is able to act, and the reaction of the etheric body is to initiate energy changes which are passed to the physical body. The mind, in fact, works through the etheric counterpart of the physical body. The latter merely reacts as an automaton to the continually changing energy currents being received. This explanation is put forward again as an hypothesis for the purpose of examining what is written in this book without continually confronting it with your own opposing views. Further experience will either confirm or reject it. It is your own mind that must be the authority you seek, and you will be in no doubt when that authority speaks. It will be either a sudden enlightenment in the form of an unequivocal acceptance, or there will be a gradual elimination of all uncertainty and doubt.

Some interesting work has been done by Dr Burr in America, which has demonstrated that the mind influences the electrical potentials of the body measured at a little distance from the skin. Different mental attitudes were found to change the potential instantaneously. We know, of course, that mental attitudes such as anxiety, fear, irritation and others can affect the body with a variety of physical ills, but no one, other than the esotericists has come up with an explanation as to how this is brought about.

The work done by Dr Burr over some thirty years, gives us a clue which I am surprised has not been taken up more generally. His main effort was in measuring the variations in electrical potential that he discovered in human beings, animals, and even in trees, and looking for their causes. He found that significant changes had taken place in diseased organs, and was able to forecast the presence of cancer of the womb long before it was clinically detected. His work shows conclusively, in my opinion, that either changes in the potentials were the cause of disease, or that the disease resulted in these changes. Either way there was established a direct connection between the potentials of the organs and tissues and their state of health.

When it was further demonstrated that an alteration in mental attitude could instantaneously be detected by changes in the electrical potential of the body, the final link between thought and physical energy seems to be clear. This work does not appear to have received the importance that, to me, it obviously deserves in offering a solution to a problem for which, until now, there has been none.

The mental tools I shall be considering in the following chapters are not new concepts. Such activities as focusing, visualizing, association, imagination etc. are generally understood and used more or less haphazardly by creative thinkers in many fields. But sufficient attention has not been given to them, neither have they been used consciously to augment the power of the mind, at least not in the context of energy transmitted by thought. It is a review of all these conditions that renders the use of the mind more effective that we shall be making together. Some of what I have to say will sound so simple as to be unworthy of attention, but be patient. The gradual practical application of these small improvements in the technique of thinking will work wonders in clarifying and directing thought and, in general, making the thinking process much more efficient. It will make it easier too, because one will learn how to avoid and overcome all those frustrations that prevent us from keeping our thinking in line with our intentions.

When we come to look at the optimum conditions in which the mind works most efficiently, and the actual ways of using it, we find that there is a clear division between the environmental conditions which I refer to as 'setting-up tools' and the using conditions, for which the term 'action tools' is appropriate. Let me explain. The most important setting-up tool for profound or prolonged thinking is relaxation, that is, complete relaxation of all physical activity and of the mind itself. Probably the most important action tool is visualization or mind-picturing; certainly, without this function of the mind, thought cannot be transformed into action. We shall see that the aids to thought I shall be describing will fall naturally into one or other of these categories. They are tools because they have to be, so to speak, attached to mind and brought into action before creative thinking starts.

The whole process of thinking needs to be approached much more methodically than it is at present. In the same way that a decorator has to go through the processes of scraping, stripping, rubbing-down, mixing, and finally painting, so there are very necessary preparatory processes to the art of thinking. The process of preparing the ground for thinking and actually putting the mind to work parallels the activities of the decorator. Each process has to be learnt thoroughly, but once learnt will become automatic and a natural part of the thinking effort. Until we do this, our thinking is bound to be interrupted, and lacking in direction and clarity.

The tools that have to be used in thinking do not make the matter burdensome; neither do they require a lot of learning, they just have to be remembered and applied. It will be found that one gets a far greater satisfaction from the thinking one has to do, and it will be done much more quickly. I hope I have been able to convince the reader that what he is going to read is relevant, is not complicated, and is practical and rewarding. With this in view, let us examine the first tool, a 'setting-up tool' — relaxation.

CHAPTER ONE
RELAXATION:
A SETTING-UP TOOL

This would seem to be such an obvious requirement for serious thinking, that some may wonder why I give it the significance of a tool. Obvious it may be but, if we come to think of it, we seldom relax consciously before we start to think out a problem, a programme, the writing of orders or instructions, drafting a speech, or whatever it is that we may have in hand. It is true that we may sink back into a comfortable chair, papers in hand, light up a pipe or cigarette (thus introducing a very common but unconscious distraction), put on a pair of soft slippers, and away we go ready to prepare a critique or a review on some matter that requires studied thought. These various actions have become habits because, over the years, we have found that we do this kind of thinking better in a comfortable chair rather than sitting at a desk, and the other details have been added because each, at some time or other, has resulted in a more restful condition in which to concentrate on the work to be done. However, it is not a consciously followed programme of relaxation, leading to as relaxed a state as possible every time you sit down to think. It is a found-by-experience substitute!

I have put relaxation as the first priority because the mind is

difficult enough to hold steady without all the distractions that
can come from a restless, uncomfortable body. When we come
on to consider concentration, we shall see that it is not as
difficult as many believe, if the right conditions are provided for
the effort. Relaxation is certainly the first essential before any
kind of concentration can be achieved. It is commonly accepted
that a relaxed mind means a relaxed body, but it is not quite so
evident that the reverse is also true. A relaxed body is free from
little muscular movements, aches and pains, tension from
muscles still being held ready for action, and all the myriad
disturbances the body can inflict on the mind. When these have
quietened down into a condition of peace and calm, then the
mind itself can relax with greater ease. One very often thinks one
is relaxed, but a cursory run over the body will reveal that there
are still areas that are tense, and muscles not properly switched
off. What we have to realise is that full relaxation, or anything
near it, will not come of its own accord; it has to be won by
practice, until it is an automatic reaction whenever one has to do
some serious thinking. There are many current instructions for
inducing a relaxed state, among which perhaps the simplest is to
imagine oneself feeling like a limp wet rag. This is on the right
lines, but it doesn't go far enough. Then there are many groups
studying fringe ideas that start their meetings with meditation
preceded by a 'led relaxation'. In this, the leader of the group for
the purpose of the meeting, takes them on an imaginary
journey, speaking aloud and describing, perhaps, a path
through a beautiful garden, or a walk by a peaceful lake. The
scene is described in some detail and each member of the group
follows with his mind-pictures making as much of the scene as
he can. It might be a scene such as the following:

You are walking down a brick path in the early evening.
There is no breeze and the air is balmy, soft, and fragrant with
the perfume of the flowers that fill the beds each side of the
path. You can see, in your mind's eye, all the flowers you are
fond of, growing in profusion with no gaps between them
where weeds can flourish. You note with some surprise that
there are flowers of all seasons in bloom; paeonies, delphin-
iums, phlox, roses, michaelmas daisies, sistus, hibiscus, and
many others, some of which you have seen but cannot name.

The path leads to a little wrought-iron gate which you open and pass through on to a soft track running through a meadow of well-trimmed grass. On the right, the ground slopes down to a small river winding its way into the far distance. Beyond this, there are mountains rising up into the snow line, their outline softened by a blue haze forming a perfect background to the meadow with its graceful trees, the meandering river, and the rich green of the valley stretching away to the foot of the mountains. You drink in the quiet and peace of the scene, and just ahead you see a seat on one side of the grassy path, inviting you to stop. You sit down and let the beauty sink into your inmost being. You feel utterly relaxed and at peace with the world. You have no worries, no problems; everything is working out for the good. You feel, too, an inner trust that this is so. You feel and welcome the inflow of the beneficial energy that pervades this secret place, and you let this energy spread through your body, your mind, and your whole being. You are utterly at peace.

This relaxation exercise lasts no more than five minutes, sufficient to lead the group away from the troubles and frustrations of their daily life, to the peace and quiet required for the meditation which follows. It is a good programme for inducing relaxation, especially for those who find it difficult to do an exercise of this sort on their own initiative. It is also an excellent introductory exercise to bring the group together in a subjective unity. This is a very important consideration, but too often forgotten. There are, however, disadvantages. It is not self-generated; it does not cover the body in any detail; it is specifically a relaxation of the body that results from relaxing the mind. In short, it is not thorough enough to produce as complete a physical relaxation as is required. The secret of conscious relaxation is the art of 'letting go'. Try this out on some particular muscle, say the biceps, which is one that nearly all people can flex and relax at will. First tense up the muscle by bending the forearm, and then gradually let the tension fall away. Straighten the arm, and with the focus held on the muscle and an act of imagination, draw all the energy from it, until it lies slack and inert on the table (the arm not the muscle!), incapable of any action until energy is once again pumped into it by an effort of will. This is what happens when we complete an action with a muscle and unconsciously relax it; the effect can be increased when it is done consciously.

This is an example of what must be done all over the body in order to make sure that all is 'let go'. That sounds rather a long and tedious effort, but it need not be so. After having practised as suggested above on one or two muscles (the main thigh muscle, the rectus femoris, is a good one to add to the biceps), a simple pattern will have been established, and it is then only necessary to run the focus over the whole body. This is done by starting at the toes and finishing at the forehead, consciously withdrawing the energy from each muscle in turn where you know a muscle to be, or from an area if you are not sure.

Your run over the body will go something like this:
Starting with the toes of both feet, then move to the instep where one very often gets cramp, the area round the heel, ankle, to the calf, the knee, thighs, front back and sides, the muscles at the waist, the stomach, back, shoulders, neck, arms, hands, fingers, jaw, ears, eyes, forehead. You can, of course, add to this list. What I have given is only a general indication of how the 'run round' is done. It only requires a focused 'glance' at each muscle or area, with the accompanying mental instruction to withdraw all the energy. There is no necessity to pause as you go. Let the survey be a slow-moving sweep, always with the idea of 'letting go' strong in the mind, so that the muscles will become completely discharged of all energy. The first time or two, it may take you three or four minutes to run from your toes to your head, but once the routine has become familiar, it should only require about one and a half minutes at the most. Until the exercise begins to feel effective, it is a good idea to run back from the head to the toes again, to make sure that all is relaxed and tensionless, but as soon as you can feel the effect all over your body, the single run will be sufficient. You will find that the process will eventually become automatic, so that as soon as you sit down for some thinking task, your subconscious mind, that willing slave, the autonomic mind that is continually working to keep your body going, will do the job for you!

This is an exercise to teach oneself the art of relaxation. It should be practised before settling down to a period of prolonged thinking about anything, even if it is only planning a holiday. As you well know, the body is a creature of habit; repeat some physical or mental action sufficiently and the mind will automatically initiate a repetition when the situation indicates that it is time for it. You will then find that, as you sit down to work, a feeling of complete relaxation will come over you. This you should acknowledge, and appreciate that you have now given the mind the most important, or one of the most important, 'setting-up tools' — a peaceful background, empty of all distracting movements and other calls of the senses for attention. It is these conscious sense responses that tend to pull the mental focus away from what it is fixed on. There is no problem about focusing, provided that the information to give it substance is there; the problem is always in keeping it steady. I shall deal with this fully later in the chapter on concentration; here I only want to bring into the open those minor and usually unobserved messages from the senses that constantly interrupt our thinking process.

We really do need to learn how to relax more often in our daily life. Just watch a cat. Even on the hunt, waiting to spring on some unsuspecting field mouse, the animal is a picture of relaxed concentrated power. Whenever it does not require energy for walking, eating, or some playful activity, its body is obviously relaxed. We should learn to be more like the cat and be less wasteful with our energy. At all times of the day, muscles are unnecessarily tense, and wasteful actions with all parts of the body are constantly being made; all these consume energy. We are very inefficient users of energy; with a little practice and attention, it could so easily become a habit to relax all those parts of the body not required for the action of the moment. The sort of relaxing exercise I have given earlier in this chapter is a good beginning. Used, at first, specifically for periods of thinking, it can quickly become a habit to shut off the pressure wherever energy is not required. This doesn't mean that it will then take longer to bring muscles into action. On the contrary, the inflow of energy will be more dynamic because of the absorbing power of the relaxed muscle, and the instruction from the mind via the brain will be more effective, because it is a 'full throttle' decision and not just a 'bit more Charlie'!

This is the first tool we must learn to use. Without it we are not giving the mind a chance. The more specialized an instrument is, the more care is required in setting-up and fitting the necessary tool. The mind is an exceptionally complex and specialized instrument, and it is surprising that we have not realised this. It is treated almost with disdain by most of us. Why? I suppose because it *seems* to work satisfactorily without us having to fuss about the conditions we expect it to work in. When working at even the mundane level of the physical world (which is only an insignificant portion of its full potential), it has the penetrating power of X-ray, the analytical, selective, and memory power of the computer, and a creative power with which we are at present only fumbling, like a child with building blocks. But there is no magic word or some simple method that will enable us to release and utilize the power that lies behind our often rambling and ill-directed thought. It is a long and patient task of learning how to give the mind the conditions it needs, of clearing away all the obstructions and obstacles to the natural flow of mental energy. That may sound too theoretical, but it is not. An electrical circuit has to be clear, that is, free from resistance, in order to allow the maximum electrical energy to pass along it. Mental energy is a finer form of electrical energy; it is therefore more easily obstructed. The smallest amelioration of these obstructing conditions will have a significant effect on the amount of energy available for the task in hand. We have begun to think in terms of energy, and mental energy works just like any other variety. Let us get that fixed in our minds right from the start. Thinking is manipulating mental energy; forming it into recognisable shapes called thought-forms, which can be seen by some gifted persons. These thought-forms, in the case of the average human being are vague, ill defined, and soon fade away.

It is fortunate that, in order to develop the power that lies latent in the mind, we require vision, determination, patience, and faith in the outcome of our efforts and, above all, time. It is fortunate, because during this time we have the opportunity and will feel the compulsion to develop our higher qualities, so that we gradually change our reaction to our fellow men and humanity at large, from one of a separative 'I'm all right Jack' attitude, to one of inclusive love and concern. This is the result of the vertical expansion of the mind that I referred to earlier. In the gradual expansions that lie before us, the mind will become more and more inclusive, inclusive of concepts of which we now have no inkling, and inclusive of those persons we formerly had excluded from our direct love.

It is this vertical expansion that will ensure that we use the enhanced powers of the mind for the general good and not for the benefit of our own personality aims. This process of learning from insight, of the essential brotherhood and unity of the human race, and indeed of all creation, is one which should proceed along with the gradual elimination of the obstacles to clear thinking that forms the subject of this book.

The complete relaxation of body and mind is the ideal to be aimed at, but do not be disappointed if it is not complete. It never will be, until the mind has left all association with physical phenomena behind, and is experiencing on the higher planes of mental awareness. Each step nearer to complete relaxation gives the mind that much more scope to attend to its own business, and not to be distracted by demands for attention that have become habitual, and which are continually fed by the senses' insistence on priority for their reports from the world of phenomena.

We are at an in-between stage, when the conflict between what is essential to spiritual and mental growth, and what has been essential to intellectual development, is revealing a dichotomy in our developing nature. It has happened before, when all those processes now carried out without our conscious knowledge by the autonomic mind, were the main occupation of conscious activity, but were gradually being handed over to the care of the subconscious. That was when the intellect was beginning to be aware of other aspects of the environment that we now call mental. In order to be able to pay attention to these, it was necessary that the previously important conscious activity should be relegated to a role of lower priority.

The human mind is at this exciting stage of its development, beginning to respond to the pull of the higher mind, with a wealth of contacts being opened up before it. This necessarily means that the previously important physical contacts must take a back seat. We can see this happening in the many cases on record of people with mental abilities that smack of the miraculous.

This acknowledgement that the mind must be given the right conditions in which to work is an affirmation that this process of expansion is understood, and will be consciously assisted.

CHAPTER TWO
CONCENTRATION:
AN ACTION TOOL

Discussion with a number of people has convinced me that there is a very great misunderstanding about what is required for concentration. It is clearly thought to be difficult to concentrate. It is not, provided the right technique is used. The rather vague association the word has is of a furrowed brow, clenched teeth, rigid and tense muscles of the head and neck, and generally a forceful expression of static physical energy. This is almost laughable, because it is the exact opposite of what concentration should be. In the previous chapter, I have explained that the full power of the mind can not be brought to bear until tension has been eliminated from all muscles and parts of the body. One has to be very careful, when intending to concentrate, that the kind of tensions I have just indicated are not set up by the very idea of concentrating!

Efficient use of the mind cannot be achieved without concentration. Many have written to me after reading my earlier book *Mind Your Body*, to say 'I can't do it because I can't concentrate.' It was this attitude which I found so common, that prompted me to include some explanation of what concentration really is in this book. It is *not* difficult if approached in the right way. Nearly everyone can concentrate without trouble when what he or she is doing is interesting.

For many people concentration is becoming aware of one's inability to keep the mind on a subject! It is not until one tries to concentrate that one becomes acutely aware of the unstable nature of the mind, with its tendency to flit from one disconnected thought to another. This started as a very natural tendency when mind was beginning to become paramount. Up to that time, the emotional and physical natures had unchallenged priority, and man was continually at the call of their demands. There must have been, at that time, much less of the uncontrolled wandering we experience today. But when mind at first began to challenge the priority of the emotional and physical natures, there was nothing yet on to which it could fasten, nothing higher in the form of abstract and conceptual thinking had so far materialized. The result has been that the emotional and physical demands for attention are still able to continue, in a less successful way, what was previously a monopoly.

Now that these calls are beginning to lose, or have already lost, their force, we are in the position of looking for new thoughts to occupy the mind's attention, and trying to compel the mind to attend to these rather than the distracting messages that continue to filter in rather haphazardly. The mind is no longer occupied with automatic responses, as it used to be with the emotional and physical bodies; it is beginning to be controlled by the 'I', which takes its ultimate authority from the soul or essence of the human being. It is this burgeoning control that is so significant and makes the situation so novel. The mind has to be taught a new role — that of being subservient and of being directed. It is simply the old habit reasserting itself that introduces all the distractions that we find when we try to concentrate or meditate. The new habit has not yet been formed, and the old, once legitimate and proper conscious contacts of the physical and emotional natures whether direct or in the form of memory, succeed in enticing the mind away from what you intend it to do. That is an interpretation of what happens when you try to concentrate, and why. It is as natural as the action of a horse resisting the bit when being broken in. Understanding the cause and knowing the remedy will remove that helpless feeling 'I can't concentrate.'

Focusing and elimination are the two main elements in concentration and there are techniques to be employed for both of these. First of all, let us look at focusing, the germ around which concentration forms. Focusing the mind is not difficult, we do this all the time; it is maintaining the focus that presents the difficulty to many people. It is essential that the subject on which we wish to focus is made as interesting as possible, so that it is necessary to prepare the ground. If it is interesting, it will attract our attention, and it is attention that keeps focus steady. Quite often the subject may be one which doesn't naturally attract our interest, in which case it must be 'researched'. By this, I don't mean the kind of research that is required for writing a book about something of which one lacks detailed knowledge, or where the knowledge one has must be filled in with information obtained from a library, or perhaps a visit to the locality concerned. I mean 'research' in a much more restricted sense. Let me give you an example. In my previous book, *Mind Your Body*, I gave programmes where it is necessary to know a little about the functioning of the body in getting rid of infection or obstructions, or of assisting the healing process of a wound. A simple mind-picture is formed of how this takes place, not necessarily with anatomical accuracy, but with sufficient detail to show the process working. This information has to be obtained either from a kindly doctor, or from a medical book such as *Gray's Anatomy*. If the information has to come from a book, then one has to be careful to abstract only the necessary detail to form a simple picture of the process one is 'researching'. The temptation to try and 'see' more than is necessary must be resisted.

It is generally necessary only to collect together the thoughts one has about the subject, or to look at the problem generally with the various alternatives that present themselves. In sifting the facts, one has to use discrimination. This is a tool of very common use. Its use is a parallel to the action of cutting out from a sheet of metal the shape that is going to be worked into the final form of the desired object. It is an act of selection and discarding, of deciding what is relevant and what is not. It is a quality of mind that has to be increasingly developed as expansion is embarked on. Behind descrimination lie all the factors that influence choice, and the light of discrimination must be used on these too. Some will be found to be emotionally generated; whenever possible discrimination should not rely on emotional colouring of the facts. It must rely on true intellectual relevance only.

This will give one a packet of information on which to work, and the more this contains, the more interesting it is likely to be. The act of focusing isolates this information from the rest of one's thinking. Imagine the mind acting as the beam of a searchlight illuminating these facts and holding them in view for detailed examination. There is no force applied to this act of focusing. The light of the mind simply illuminates. As one begins to analyse the information under scrutiny, so the process of elimination becomes the critical agent in maintaining the focus. This, again, is a gentle process, one of fending off intruding thoughts of all kinds. These will *always* appear. People frequently speak of 'making their mind a blank', but I don't believe this is possible except for those far advanced in mental control. Intruding thoughts will always attempt to interrupt; the secret is not to allow them the energy they need to break the train of thought. They must be brushed off, not aggressively or with irritation, but gently and firmly. They must be treated in a way that deflates them, so that they fade away and die from lack of attention. Suppose the thought of a party you are giving the next day, and the catering and preparing that must be done before it, appears uninvited in your mind, or the rememberance of something you ought to have done earlier in the day; deal with it in the following manner. Shift your focus momentarily to the thought; label it as 'planning' or 'remembering', or maybe just 'wandering'. Whatever it is, attach a mental label that will give it a 'pigeonhole' into which it will fit, and then switch your focus back to the matter on which you have been concentrating. You will find that this *will* deflate the thought and abstract the energy from it. Sometimes a thought will come into the mind that is more persistent. In this case, hold the focus on it while you follow it to its conclusion. In the thought of the forgotten action mentioned above, think 'all right I'll do it this evening', or however you propose to handle it, and then return your focus to the matter in hand. This is a trick that I was taught by my meditation master in Burma, and which is referred to in *An Experiment in Mindfulness*. It is commonly used in meditation to still the chattering mind which is the greatest difficulty a beginner has to face. Introducing a method like this is an effective way of 'doing something about it' and the results are quickly apparent to the meditator.

Where one has a packet of information for the mind to dwell on, this method of warding off intruders is additionally effective, because there is so much for the mind to hold on to, as opposed to meditation, when one is usually reducing the content of mind to the absolute minimum. It will soon be found that interruptions will become less and less, all without the sense of frustration or annoyance that usually accompanies this problem.

In order to focus one needs attention, and the ability to 'attend' varies with individuals. It can only be cultivated by making what is being attended to interesting; it can't be cultivated by trying to force the mind to stay put.

This is what concentration really is, the combination of two mental activities. First focusing, which restricts attention to what is to be investigated, and then the elimination of interruptions. Tackled in this way, it soon becomes possible to hold the focus steady as long as one wants. The secret is to replace the feeling of having to use force with this simple method. Concentration will come naturally if the right conditions are there. It only appears difficult because of the constant stream of interrupting thoughts that take one's attention away from the subject to be studied. If one is seriously lacking in the ability to concentrate, this will not be overcome at once, but gradually; as the system of fending off intruding thoughts becomes a habit, the steadiness of one's focus will improve perceptibly and one will realise 'I *can* concentrate!'. It is rather like learning to ski. One can't ski until one has learnt all the tricks of leaning the weight, bending the knees, or whatever the current training fad happens to be. The difference is that one knows that one cannot ski without training and practice, but one thinks one can concentrate, or ought to be able to, without taking the trouble to learn!

Concentration is the second most important tool that the mind uses in getting force into its thinking. It should be taught, and one can imagine interesting ways in which this could be done. A group of students would be given a subject to study and instructed how to deal with any interruptions that will inevitably occur. These could be introduced by the teacher in the form of sudden noises, flashing lights, pleasant or unpleasant smells, or anything that would be sure to get the attention of the students. It would be up to them to see how quickly they were able to banish the thought of the interruption from their minds, and would be an amusing game for them.

The use of most of the tools I shall be writing about could be taught by quite simple methods. It really is rather surprising that, knowing the potential of the mind even as we do, we do nothing to increase the power of thinking; all we generally do is to increase the *amount* of thinking that has to be done.

As a setting-up tool, these two functions of focusing and elimination together give the mind that continued stable environment that it requires. All its available energy can then be expended on the thinking that has to be done, and not wasted on all those extraneous thoughts that, at present, are given too easy access.

CHAPTER THREE
ASPIRATION, FAITH, CONFIDENCE, CONVICTION: A PROGRESSIVE SETTING-UP TOOL

These are all attitudes of mind. The four words indicate the extent to which it is possible to clear a path for the transmission of mind-directed energy. As such they together represent a vital tool of the mind, one of which we should be conscious, and which we should learn to cultivate in order to convert faith into conviction and realization. Aspiration is a long term attitude; it is the result of a distant vision of something to be achieved. It is a spur to continued effort and contains within it the hope and promise of success. The first taste of experience will convert aspiration into faith, and with further experience this will become confidence. It is when confidence has been proved and justified by further experience that conviction is won. New knowledge is gained in this way. By any other way it is second-hand. All these attitudes of mind have progressively increasing effect on the transmission of energy by thought.

'Energy follows thought' is a quotation often used by those studying esoteric philosophy and psychology. It is a short sentence but it packs a punch. First of all, it infers that thought is a substance, not the sort of substance we call tangible, but of a finer nature scientists have yet to discover. The statement means that, where thought is directed, there energy will find its target. It doesn't mean that energy follows *after* thought, but that wherever thought is trained, there will energy be directed. It means, too, that we cannot think without having some effect of good or evil that is as real and positive as a punch on the nose! Few people attach that significance to their thinking. The more general attitude is 'I can get away with a thought of harming someone or even of murdering them, provided that it is only a thought.' But that is far from the truth. The energy of hate has been transmitted with the thought and it will unerringly find its objective. It won't, of course, result in immediate physical action, though where the energy is intense, as it is in the case of the witch doctors of western Africa, physical harm can result in a matter of hours or days. I spent some years on the west coast and learnt from the District Commissioners there of the very real power these men wield, one which, at that time, there was no means of countering. I don't know whether the new rulers of these territories have found in their own way the trick of deflecting the power that the witch doctors direct mostly for their own selfish ends. The certain way to overcome unwelcome thought-charged energy that has 'locked-on' to a human being is, of course, to dissipate it with a love-charged thought of the same power. The trouble is that few of us are able to raise love to the all-embracing level that will give it the necessary power. Neither do we, as yet, possess the focusing power of the mind to form a sufficiently clear channel along which this love energy can be directed.

You may well be thinking 'what has all this to do with the subject of the chapter?' These progressively positive attitudes of mind, aspiration, faith, confidence, and conviction, determine the degree to which energy can be carried by the thought they are supporting. We well know that this can drastically affect our physical actions. To lack confidence is to be hesitant, timid, faltering, and undecided. If, for instance, you are asked to make a speech and it is something you are not accustomed to doing, it would be wise to build up your confidence by making yourself fully conversant with the subject of the speech, and to rehearse it until you are sure that you will be able to speak freely and in a convincing manner.

Or, if you are being physically attacked, and cringe away

pathetically from each blow, or take a somewhat more aggressive attitude, but halfheartedly, believing that you are going to come off second best, that is just what will happen. But if your attitude of mind is strongly aggressive, even if you have no plan of how to deal with the situation, your physical actions will match your mood, and your attacker will realize that he has a tough fight on his hands.

It is always the attitude of mind that makes for a resisting or a conducting channel through which thought has to travel. We have a parallel in the strength of an electric current which depends on the resistance of the circuit through which it passes. This fact, when we become aware of it, has an important lesson for us in the way that we do things. There is no sense in doing anything with a grudging attitude. If it is going to be done, then it should be done with the attitude expressed by one of the words heading this chapter. This applies as much to letting a friend use your tennis racquet or other very personal possession, as to granting permission to someone to camp in your garden. Either do it with good grace, or don't do it.

You may not agree with the order in which I have placed the words that we are looking at, but between confidence and conviction there is a gradual shading of attitude to what might be called a 'clear circuit'. This clear circuit is only obtained when the attitude of conviction leads to knowledge, not the knowledge that stems from information, but the knowledge that comes from the higher reaches of the mind itself, that we speak of as the intuition. Intuition presents us with insight that is very different to anything reached through analytical or rational processes. It is, if you like, soul knowledge, but I hesitate to use the word 'soul' as it means so many different things to different people. It is, in effect, knowledge that feeds down into the brain from a part of the mind that is not concerned with the goings-on of the personality. But we have ourselves to build the circuit that will enable the transmissions to reach the lower mind and thence the brain.

The building of this bridge is the process which leads to the integration of the personality with the essence of one's being, represented by the word 'soul'. Knowledge, of course, even intuitional knowledge, always has to be interpreted, and this requires the use of the lower mind and the brain. For this use to be efficient, both mind and brain require training, and this is where education comes in. The process of thinking must be clear and cover a wide field, and the reaction of the brain must be sufficient to make the ideas of practical value in daily living. It is the brain, as the end of the process, that has the job of converting ideas into physical action.

There must be a school of learning before the school of wisdom can be attained. That is why the educational system is of such paramount importance for the spiritual development of the race. The aim of education must always be the achievement of wisdom. This comes from absorbing, leading to understanding, to interpreting in action, followed by a repetition of the process on a higher level. At present, education is directed more or less solely to success in gaining a living and becoming a cog in the material aspect of living. It should be much more than this; its main direction should always be towards developing the full potential of the human being at all its different levels, giving the purely material aspect its right and proper significance, but not to emphasize it to the disadvantage of the much more valuable aim of the expansion of consciousness. It is this expansion that will eventually lead earthbound man to become a member of the kingdom of God. That is not just a pious-sounding phrase; it is the state of man when he is ruled and directed by his pure essence, his soul.

I know there are some who are trying to do just this, and it is hoped that they will point the way to all those who are concerned with the education of the world's young, as well as all those who are not too old to learn. The kingdom of God must become a generally accepted aim, and it must have precise meaning. In contrast, the kingdom of man is ruled by the personality; because of this it is separative and in its lowest form, entirely selfish. It is mind that enters the kingdom of God when it learns to handle the personality as the field for the expression of the inner man, the Christian soul, and the Buddhist essence of mind. When the last vestige of control by the personality has been replaced by the pure light of soul illuminating the mind and thus influencing the brain, then man has entered the kingdom of God.

One doesn't have to be physically dead to do this. On the contrary, one must do it while physically alive, because it is then, and only then, that the battle with the personality can take place. As a member of the kingdom of God, man's whole attitude to his fellow men and to creation as a whole, has become all inclusive, dominated by love, and the petty interests of the personality have dropped below the level of consciousness.

I know that it is difficult to appreciate such a state as one to look forward to; one is too fond of one's personality, and at present it seems to be all we have to hang on to. To lose it seems too much like ceasing to be. That is a very valid reflection and one which cannot be fully overcome until an alternative is clear before our mind. This alternative will surely open up. It is part of the next expansion of consciousness to reveal the reality of a higher sense of self and, in contrast, the unreality of the personality concept.

But to return to the four words regarded in the sense of 'setting-up tools'. They represent mental attitudes that are the hallmark of the fully committed man or woman, and I mean fully committed to his or her actions in the varying degrees that the words imply. You will note that confidence is somewhat less effective than conviction in charging thought with energy; it brings experience and then the knowledge that will lead to conviction. But it is a very powerful medium for bringing the creative imagination into action. Blind unquestioning faith, the kind that led African warriors to consider themselves immune to the bullets of the white man, is a form of wishful thinking as we understand the word, (not as it really should be understood). Faith has to be built up and tested through experience. Self-test is the one test we have that is first hand. If I tell you that eating lettuce will turn you green, and you believe me to be an honest and truthful man, you might be tempted to have faith in what I say, and either eat lettuce or not, depending on whether you wished to turn green or remain as you are! In this case, where a self-test is precarious, it would be wise to seek further information about the matter. This is clear in this particular case, but when the faith concerns a more abstract element of belief, and one that cannot be self-tested without a long period of trial, we are tempted to let our emotions lead us into acceptance, rather than encourage the rational part of the mind to have its say. One should never make decisions on emotion alone; be influenced, yes, but not swayed. The human personality is (or should be), a unified triple vehicle, physical, emotional and mental, and, in any decision, each should be given its due share where it is applicable.

Faith *must* be tempered with reason, particularly in these days when the miracles of science are our everyday experience. Anything is possible, very probably; but anything goes, certainly not. Sometimes the conclusion one way or another is assisted by an intuitional spark which has filtered down from the higher mind, and one should always be ready to recognize it, however low on the spiritual ladder one may feel oneself to be.

There are traps all along the way from aspiration to conviction, of course. There are too many fanatics about, who have failed to test each stage of progression towards conviction. Wide-eyed acceptance of what one is being led into or taught, is not the way a mature individual should react, and it is not what we have a mind for. The mind is always available to penetrate to new knowledge. The old attitude 'we are not meant to know about that', is just as bad as the fanatical reaction brought about by inadequate use of the mind. The mind is capable of all knowledge, but not now, not yet.

Aspiration is the first shape of this tool that we are able to discern. It grows apace, is unobtrusive, and its fervour is gentle and hidden. As the gradual expansion into faith takes place, there is the danger of believing one has reached the end of the road; all is settled and sure, and others must be told, be persuaded to follow. This is the beginning of fanaticism. It must be warded off by the determination to await further experience. This, if it confirms what faith is presenting, should bring with it a sense of balance — what is for me may not be suitable for all. Faith must be lived with first as a personal discovery, and later as a shared working hypothesis. As it gradually builds into confidence, its scope can be enlarged without aggressive interference in others' beliefs. Example must always come first; the rest will follow naturally. Between confidence and conviction there must be a great cleaning-out, a purification of motive so that no shred of the lower man, represented by the personality, will be in a position to override the decisions coming from the higher mind. These, of course, have to be channelled through the lower mind, and performed by the personality. Because of this, the personality must always retain the significance of the doer. It is, after all, the vehicle through which the essence that constitutes man gains its experience. But once conviction has been won, the voice of personality must lose its strident nature and become less demanding. Finally, as children were exhorted in my younger days to be seen and not heard, it must be seen to be doing what soul requires, and with voice reduced to acquiescence. Sounds depressing, this deflation of the personality? We have to face up to the fact that it has to be reduced to something more like the stomach, silent (except when protest is necessary), and willing!

Conviction is only free from all personality taints when it is illuminated by the light from the essence of one's being. It is another way of describing intuitional knowledge, that which we should now be preparing ourselves to receive.

CHAPTER FOUR
VISUALIZATION OR
MIND-PICTURING:
AN ACTION TOOL

This is a very important 'action tool'. It is one that we use consciously, but when associated with physical action, its use is mostly subconscious. Because of this, we do not realize how essential it is for any creative activity of the mind.

The action tools are those that we have to select for the various kinds of thinking we have to do. Some of these we make use of consciously because we have learnt or been taught to think in that way. But others we use quite unconsciously, having gradually developed them through experience. It will come as a surprise to learn that they could be regarded as anything other than normal thinking habits. But tools they are; means the mind makes use of to extract or retain information that would otherwise not be available, and to increase the energy that a thought will carry.

The tool I want to discuss in this chapter is visualization or mind-picturing. It is important because it is essential for all creative mental action, and for all physical response. The art of mind-picturing is of far greater importance than most of us give it credit for, and the ability to visualize varies considerably with individuals. It was a long time before I understood that this is the case. I remember that when I was doing my sublieutenant's technical courses in electricity, gunnery, and navigation, we had to reproduce a lot of technical drawings or portions of charts. Some had no difficulty whatever in doing this, but I found it a tiresome slog. A particular friend of mine was able to look at a quite complicated drawing for only a minute or so, and then reproduce it with accuracy. The consequence to me was that I did badly in all the exams that required drawings to support the text. Visualization can, of course, be cultivated by practice. The ability is there. This is demonstrated clearly in our dreams, which involve the most intricate mind-picturing in very great detail. When we dream of people, their faces are distinct and recognizable, but if I try to picture my wife's face in my mind's eye, I cannot reproduce the detail that I do in a dream. It only needs practice, therefore, to transfer this ability from the subconscious to the conscious mind. This creative ability of the mind doesn't stop there; we can also reproduce the products of the other four senses in the form of 'think-hear', 'think-feel', 'think-smell', and 'think-taste'. How often have we found it difficult to get a tune out of our mind? A composer writes down the sounds that he hears in his mind, and Benjamin Britten used to write the orchestrations of his compositions in his mind on the way up to London in the train.

These interpretations which we sense as sight, hearing, smell, taste, and touch, are the mind's reaction to different vibrations that are received via the sense organs. It is the mind that turns them into the physical impressions of sight, hearing, etc. Along the road from the sense organs, the vibrations have been converted into electrical energy pulses, and it is these that the mind transforms into the colours and substances of our physical world. It should be simple and natural for us to think our sense responses without the help of the sense organs, but few of us are able to do this with all of them. Some, like me, are bad at all of them, with the exception of those that are required to initiate physical action, or the simplest of activities of the other senses, such as humming a tune in one's mind, or thinking of the taste of a banana! One should be able to 'think-see', 'think-hear', 'think-smell', 'think – taste', and 'think – feel' at will, with as much accuracy as the senses will give one. Once the mind has reacted to any particular range of these pulses, and interpreted them as the sense which they initiate, it should obviously be able to reproduce this purely mental result without requiring the initial stimulus given by the sense organ.

During infancy, the mind gradually builds up experience of its interpretation of the messages received from the senses. Of these, the sense that dominates the activities of the mind of the growing infant is sight. With the ability to interpret these messages in terms of physical reality, comes also the ability to reproduce them in the mind in the form of 'think-see' etc. The faculty of making mind pictures, after being used consciously for all the experimental physical actions made by the child, is gradually taken over by the subconscious, so that common actions become automatic, as soon as the decision to undertake them has been made. These various sense impressions are what the child has to draw on as he gradually pieces them together to form his environment.

Unfortunately, most of us continue to be dominated by the endless flow of impressions from the senses. We become 'locked-on' to these, so that the mind is obstructed from receiving other messages coming from its own level. We have to teach the mind to function independently of the senses — this is what the practice of meditation does — and this will allow us to begin the search for higher levels of communication. We are then entering a school of learning which is properly the subject of esoteric philosophy and psychology, for which many books are available. Amongst the most complete are those published by the Lucis Trust under the name of Alice Bailey. Here, I am only interested in the functioning of mind before we embark on the expansions which serious esoteric study will bring about.

In order to increase the reach and efficiency of our minds at our present stage of development, there is no doubt that the cultivation of mind-picturing and the tieing-in of these pictures to the direction of energy by thought, is of paramount significance. As we climb up the ladder of expanding awareness, more and more will mind-picturing be required, in order to bring into practical use the powers of creativity that will be opening up before us.

There are, of course, many exercises designed to improve the ability of making and holding pictures in the mind; it is very often the holding of the picture steady, as though it were framed in physical substance, that is the difficulty, as indeed it was with me. One finds that one can, for instance, flash a picture say, of a friend's face or that of wife or husband, but to hold it there and fill in the details is impossible. The face is only vaguely a face, with the features roughly sketched in. Not so the artist, who must be able to hold the vision for detailed study long enough for him to put it down on canvas. I have a picture of a seascape showing the conclusion of a storm, painted without ship or shore or seabird, just a menacing, cruel sea. The size of the waves is such that it could not have been painted from life. The artist must have had the most exceptional ability to retain the details of the depth of the swell, the direction of the williwaws, and the scurrying low cloud, sufficiently to allow him to build up a lifelike picture on his canvas. The artist, one would imagine, must have a much greater power to visualize than his non-artistic fellows; and so must the composer have a greater ability for 'sound-thinking'. It is because these men have the ability to create mental images or reproductions of what their senses convey to them, that they have become artists in their particular field. The creative cook and the producer of perfumes are just as much artists as the painter, the composer, and the sculptor, in so far as their creations stem from imaginary productions of the reports of their senses.

When I use the word visualization, I include the same mind functions of all the other senses. But it is hardly possible for a person to bring all these functions of the mind to as high a degree of utilization as one can with the function of 'think-see'. This is because we use 'think-see' so generally and consistently without realising it. To take a simple example: consider a person walking up a flight of steps. For each step he takes, he has to see in his mind's eye the amount the foot must be lifted to carry it up to the level of the next step. This done, he can then give the mental instructions to the muscles to raise the foot just that amount. For each step up he takes, he must first visualize the action necessary. Although it seems to us to be 'instinctive', without the instructions based on the subconscious 'seeing' of the action being carried out, the foot could not be moved as required to clear the step. Every moment of the waking day, we are using this tool of mind-picturing, but subconsciously.

We produce all the end-products of our senses in dreaming

and, when we awake, we don't seem to find that extraordinary. This dreaming ability demonstrates that the mind is perfectly capable of reproducing all that the senses reveal with great accuracy, when it is not overshadowed by the conscious mind. Something in the activity of the conscious mind interferes with the production of mind-pictures. It is, in fact, a natural function of the mind that apparently doesn't need training. But we have to train the conscious mind to stop the continual interruptions that shut it out. The ability is there, but the environment we give the mind does not allow freedom for pure mental creation. Subconscious mental creation does not seem to be inhibited in the same way, since we make use of mind-picturing in all our physical actions. It is only when some of us try to do this consciously that we fail.

If we are to increase our mental powers, it is essential that we develop the ability to visualize. Here is an example of how one appears to have a good memory. Somebody gives you verbal instructions for finding a friend's house that you have never before visited. 'Turn right at the end of this stretch of road, continue until you see a garage on your left and turn left just beyond it. The road then twists a lot and after a few of these turns, you will pass a large pond on your right. A couple of hundred yards further on you will see a white gate on the right; that is 'Five Meadows' where your friend lives.' If you just listen to this instruction, you will certainly get lost before you are half way there; but if you make a vivid mind-picture of the route, you will have no difficulty in finding the way. That is also a very good example of the sort of practice that will develop the ability to 'see' in the mind.

It is a good plan to start consciously using the technique of mind-picturing whenever it can be applied. This avoids having to set aside special periods for practice, which many people find tiresome, and are unable to fit into their daily routine. Mind-picturing is of the greatest possible value in training the mind to be more efficient. It is the mind's most essential tool, even in our everyday thinking and actions; but when it comes to directing energy through thought, or reaching for the expansion of mind that lies next ahead for us, without visualization we cannot make progress.

If any of my readers have read of the meditation forms used in

Tibetan Tantric Buddhism, they will have learnt of the most complex and unusual mind-pictures on which the meditator is required to focus. These include details of the various gods (representing human qualities), often sitting on top of one's head, the colours of their vestments, the shape and colour of articles being held in each hand etc. For a European, even with good mind-picturing ability, these forms are very difficult to master.

Since this ability to visualize is so important in all our daily activities, I wondered how a person who had been blind from birth managed, what sense or senses took over the role played by sight in a normal person. I was able to discuss this matter with Mrs B., who had been blind all her life, and was now coming up to sixty. It was quite difficult to get her to explain how, for instance, she managed to walk up a stairway she hadn't before encountered. At first all she could reply to my questions was 'by instinct', but I persisted by putting questions as to how she actually made the necessary movements. This is what I gathered.

For the first few times, she has to check the height of each step with her stick, until she has subconsciously registered the amount of muscle movement required to lift the leg the exact distance. Then she does it, as she says, by instinct, but in fact, by a continuing accurate judgement of the amount of muscle movement that is necessary. The same kind of reaction takes place when she goes to open a door. The steps from her chair to the door again are made 'by instinct', but in reality by counting them subconsciously. Then, if it is a familiar door, she has to 'think-feel' the amount of muscle action necessary to stretch her arm out the right amount to grasp the handle. For 'think-see' with a sighted person, substitute 'think-feel' for the blind.

I checked this contention with Mrs B. by placing my hand flat on the table at a little distance from where she was sitting. I then lifted her hand and put it on top of mine. She then replaced her hand on her lap, and from there tried to put it once again on top of mine. For the first three times she made mistakes by underreaching, but the error was less each time. Finally, at the fourth attempt she was able to put her hand confidently and exactly on top of mine.

This 'sensing' required by a blind person is, in a way, less complicated than the action required of sighted persons. In the latter case, it is the eyes which subconsciously measure the distance the foot or arm must move, and this eye-distance has to be translated by the mind into the muscle movement that is necessary.

The dreams of a blind person are very limited in comparison with those of one with normal vision. They are unable to reproduce their environment other than by sounds and remembered distances. Suppose a blind person hears the front door bell in his dream, and goes to find out who is there. The sound of the bell presents no difficulty, but getting to the door is a matter of the subconscious memory of the distance, as interpreted by the number of leg muscle actions necessary to go from his chair to the door. The blind persons I spoke to all dreamt very little. One of them who had also been blind from birth, told me that her most vivid dream was of a dog she was fond of who had died. She dreamt that the dog was beside her, and when I asked her how she knew this, she replied because she could hear the sort of grunting he used to make when he was happy. She could also feel his coat when she stretched out her hand towards the sound. I think their dreams *must* be far less rich than ours; Mrs B. told me she had never had a nightmare, so that is one compensation!

It is clear to me from the short time I had for this discussion, that a person blind from birth makes use of muscle feel for getting about where we use subconscious visualization. I suspect, however, that after we have made the initial movements by the aid of visualization, with repetition, muscle feel gradually takes over. Those who have at one time been able to see, continue to visualize when they are blind, but they gradually substitute the 'think-feel' process, as the memory of vision begins to fade and the reality of muscle-feel takes over. But they all said that they dreamt much as they did before they were blind.

Our dreams are dominated by the sense of sight, and they are normally built round a pictured scene; but the blind person without special qualifications such as being musical, or perhaps a blender of perfumes, has less to act as a regular foundation for his dreams. He must depend largely on 'think-hear'.

One has always heard that the senses of a blind person are

more acute than those of a normal person, but this is usually taken to refer to the sense of hearing. It is apparent, from what I was told, that the sense of feel is perhaps predominant in their lives; it certainly replaces in all their physical actions the visualization that we use. Together, the enhanced sense of feeling and of hearing make up for much that they have lost with the sense of sight. 'Think-hear' and 'think-feel' share the dominance in their lives which, for those who see, is held by 'think-see'.

There is no doubt that the mental impression of what a sense reveals will fade after a while, if the sense is not functioning. I have an example of this in my own loss of taste and smell. This happened some twenty years ago, and a few tastes remained clear in my mind for some years, so that I could imagine what my food tasted like; if my 'think-taste' had been strong enough, I should have been able to replace what my physical sense was depriving me of. Gradually the remembrance of the various tastes faded so that I was no longer able to reconstruct in my mind what my food should taste like. Ideally, with the loss of a sense like that, one should be able to affix to one's food whatever taste one wished. I think that I probably did this for some years, but gradually the ability has faded out.

In my previous book *A Manual of Self-Healing*, I gave programmes that required simple visualization, so that the mind could pass instructions to the autonomic mind, that part of the subconscious that directs all the processes of the body including those that are functioning all the time in maintenance and healing. The visualizing technique is used too, if one wants to direct energy to any part of the body. The energy has to be seen as flame-coloured light flowing to and flooding the area where it is required. With the combination of a mental instruction and the accompanying mind-picture, energy will be delivered to the desired spot. This is a valid way of using the mind of which many are unaware.

In the search for the essence of mind itself, a search which seeks the conscious awareness of this essence (whether you call it 'soul' or 'pure mind'), it is mind-picturing that leads the way. Picture to yourself something you haven't got but could have, and wish to have, and you are on your way to getting it. This is a rough description of the 'as if' principle which I shall be discussing later. The mind sets the desired picture, thought directs the energy, and inevitably the result will appear in physical shape. It won't be instantaneous, it may take a little while, depending on the strength of the picture and the purity of the mental focus, but it will come. The power of energy-charged thought is irrisistible. There will come a time when mind-power on this scale will be used consciously to transform ideas into active organisations, and to build the forms of which the creative mind has produced the blueprints.

This is the practical 'doing' aspect of the reaching out for new awareness, and must parallel the inward probing action of the mind. Each step that is made towards a higher awareness has to be matched by the practical application of the new knowledge that the step brings with it. This includes a more embracing view of one's fellow men, and a stilling of criticism and hurtful actions of all kinds.

It is not easy to match high aspiration with equivalent thoughts and deeds. It certainly can't be done without 'taking thought'. Here again, conscious mind-picturing can take the initiative. One can ensure that, in picturing one's fellow men, one does it in as kindly a light as possible, despite their shortcomings. Such a mind-picture will influence your subsequent actions. In many little ways you can put your good intentions into mind-pictures first; if you do, you will find that you will gradually learn to follow these in your speech and actions.

What can I say that will be of practical use to all those who don't consciously use mind-picturing, and to those who find the simplest picture difficult to hold steady? The first encouragement I can offer is that practice will improve the ability in a quite startling manner. When starting off, don't be too ambitious. I was content with pictures of line-drawing simplicity. Concentrate on holding the picture steady. As you become aware of improvement, you can tackle more difficult pictures. Try to recall the face of your husband or wife after he or she has left the room. Include details of the various features; you may not be able to do this at first, and all you may be able to hold is a vague outline and a general recognition. If that is so, start with one feature, say the eyes, and each time you form the picture, try to see them in your memory as you do with your physical eyes. Don't be impatient if progress is slow. It will gradually become easier and you will find yourself automatically forming mind-pictures as you follow your daily activities. Remember all the time that you *have* the ability; your dreams prove this, it is only a question of realizing it consciously. Increase in mental power is brought about by persistence with some simple exercise such as this, but persistence is the key word, and it helps immensely if it is backed up by aspiration, faith, and confidence.

If you are a meditator, mind-picturing will help you in most forms, but not if you are using a mantram, such as with TM, which usually has no intellectual meaning. Mind-picturing is a basic element in esoteric meditation and it becomes more and more important as progress is made.

This habit of mind-picturing is the next stage of mental development that we must acquire before we can proceed further in opening up the vast reaches of the higher mind. We shall then understand and be able to use as a normal part of our daily life, the senses that are now referred to as paranormal. What we have discovered so far are just faint glimpses of what is waiting to be revealed.

It is because of its significance in opening up aspects of the mind that will bring the paranormal into the realm of the normal, that I have given mind-picturing a high priority in the list of the 'action tools' of the mind. It is the tool that will enable the mind to advance in controlled and steady steps. It is not a fanciful concept; it is essentially practical and life-fulfilling.

It is probable that, as we learn to reproduce the products of the senses with greater accuracy and facility, the sense reports themselves will lose their particular significance, and be relegated to the position of subconscious reaction to the environment for our wellbeing and safety. We shall no longer be titillated as we are now, for we shall be able to produce all that the senses can give us without their aid, and reaction to the senses will become more automatic than it already is.

CHAPTER FIVE
BREATHING:
A SETTING-UP TOOL

The way in which we breathe is an important tool for general thinking, and a vital one for certain rather restricted uses of the mind. I have written about this fairly fully in my previous book *A Manual of Self-Healing*, but because it is of considerable importance and interest, I am repeating the information here for the benefit of those who have not read the earlier book.

Two very important uses for this tool are meditation and healing, and these use the tool for directly opposed reasons. For the first, energy is being directed inwards, and for healing, it is being directed outwards to one's own body or that of a patient.

The way in which we breathe can increase quite remarkably the amount of energy the mind is able to direct to its object. The converse is also true, that wrong breathing will reduce the amount of energy transmitted to a minimum.

In normal breathing, we have four distinct periods of lung activity. First, inhalation; following this there is a slight pause between inhalation and exhalation. This is almost imperceptible when the breathing is even and undisturbed by mental or physical reactions. But in the kind of breathing that aims at maximum energy direction, this pause or interlude between breathing in and out is very important. After the pause comes the exhalation, followed by another pause equally impercept-ible in regular relaxed breathing. But this interlude also has its special function in energy breathing. By energy breathing I mean breathing accompanied by a mental instruction or proposition, with the intention of bringing into action the creative imagination. Normal unconscious breathing by itself does not have this effect; its function is limited to exercising the muscles operating the lungs and increasing the oxygen available to the blood, but breathing accompanied by conscious mental activity becomes a wielder of energy of untold power and effect. Let us consider the breathing cycle taking each of the four actions in turn, and discussing the particular role each plays in the direction and distribution of energy.

Breathing in
This, in the case of healing, is the period of setting the scene where the action is to take place, the area of the body that requires healing, and the cells, arteries, organs etc. that will have to take action. It can be compared to the period before the shooting of a film scene starts, when all the necessary scenery, actors, extras etc., are warned to get ready for action. No mental order or instruction is generally given during this period other than a preparatory warning, which is usually the simple use of 'attention'. This is similar to the warning given over the loud-speakers in a warship by an officer before making an important announcement. It is prefixed by 'D'ye hear there?', followed by a pause long enough for men to switch off the tool they might be using, or stop any noisy activity. The mental instruction 'attention phagocytic cells', or 'attention bone-marrow cells' does just this.

In the case of meditation, the period of inbreathing is used for stating the condition you are relying on the creative imagination to produce as though it already existed. It might be a change of attitude, or behaviour, or a reaching of the mind towards a higher awareness. This is expressed as a quality the meditator already has acquired. It is a setting of the desired scene and should be accompanied by a mind-picture.

Upper Interlude

This quiet, still period, which may last from a second to as much as ten seconds, is used to reinforce the scene present in consciousness in order to stabilise its reality. It is a kind of director's view when all has been assembled and is ready for the cameras to roll. Errors of positioning of the actors can be checked and remedied if necessary. This corresponds to going over the scene in the body and reviewing the mustered cells waiting for your order. In meditation, it is used to add purposive aspiration to the creative action of the imagination. It is a kind of fine-tuning, of more precise focusing, so that the impact of the executive order to follow will reach the right actors in the right scene. The effectiveness of the mental order giving the instructions for the action to be taken depends on the thoroughness with which this preparatory check has been carried out.

Breathing out

This is the executive period of the breathing cycle. It is obviously so from the use we make of breathing in speaking. The greater the expulsion of breath, the more force there is behind the order being given. In healing, during this period, the instruction is given to the cells, arteries, capilliaries, organs, or areas where trouble exists. For instance, an instruction would be given to phagocytic cells to remove infected, fibrous, or calcified tissue; this is the 'get cracking' order to do the job that healing requires.

In meditation, the executive period of the cycle is used somewhat differently. It is during this period that the meditator sees and feels himself in action with the desired quality, which may be loving his fellow men, being dispassionate, resisting the demands of the lower self, or whatever it might be that the creative imagination is proposing. It is a period of interpreting in the mind the actual behaviour in daily life in which the desired quality will result. In his visualization, he sees the quality as having been acquired, and demonstrates the various ways of expressing it. This is an action picture.

Lower Interlude

This is again a period of reinforcement. In healing, one sees the action continuing and resulting in the desired effect. If this is the removal of infection from a part of the body, the picture will show the part completely healed and looking normal. This gives the autonomic mind a preview of what is being aimed at: 'this is what your completed job should look like'. It gives a positive finishing touch to the cycle of mental activity. The interludes must not be longer than can be held comfortably; three or four seconds is probably enough in healing, but longer periods are sometimes indicated in meditation, when they could be as long as twelve seconds. The meditator must, however, be careful not to attempt too long a period for these interludes, as it would inevitably upset the evenness of his breathing and he will become out of breath. In meditation, the lower interlude is similarly used to show the result in practice of the quality that is being created. If, for instance, the meditation is aimed at unifying the three bodies of expression, physical, emotional, and mental, with the 'resident', the real 'I', then during the lower interlude, the mind will hold the impression of these bodies responding and reacting as one to the directions of the enlightened 'resident'. This is a fairly difficult abstract concept, as is so much of 'targeted' meditation; but the mind is very versatile when directed with determination, and a mental feeling of this fusion will develop with practice. Both in healing and meditation, it is during this interlude that the mind-picture shows the work of the creative imagination being successfully concluded. In both, it is essentially a period of reinforcement.

In all these periods, the mental instructions are combined with forceful mind-picturing; it is this combination that produces the energy that the mind will direct. The breathing acts as a kind of conveyor belt that increases the energy – carrying capacity of thought. There are, of course, uses for this function of breathing other than healing and meditation, but these two are good examples of the way in which the tool can be used and cover all the other possible uses.

Breathing has such an obviously important function for the life of the body, that it is not surprising that we have missed the role it should play in directing thought. We do, however, appreciate that it is connected with thought, that a period of quiet even breathing will calm a disturbed mind, and that, when in a temper, breathing becomes agitated. This should have indicated to us that breathing and thought are vitally connected.

It is because we have not understood that thought is a physical substance, (though one we cannot sense with any of our physical senses, much as some gases are) that we have not considered it as a carrier of energy. But anyone listening to a speaker with 'fire in his belly' such as Hitler or Churchill and many others, would realise that such speakers control a force which affects their hearers mentally, emotionally, and frequently physically. I once heard Hitler speak to a large crowd in a field outside Darmstadt in Germany, and though, at the time, I could understand only very little German, I could feel the force he was projecting into the crowd, and I was, with them, swayed to a fervour of wholehearted agreement with what he was saying, whatever it was! That is nothing else than energy being directed by thought. Loud speech itself is not enough to influence a crowd; you can shout, and leave a listener unimpressed by what you are shouting about. You have to believe sincerely and forcefully in what you are saying. It is the belief behind the speech that loads the thought with energy, and it is the energy carried by the thought that charges the speech so that it reaches and affects the listener.

In this kind of forceful speechmaking, breathing is, of course, important. Subconsciously, such a speaker puts across those points in his speech that he wants his audience to accept as their own, with a strong expulsion of breath. Those which are explanatory, or about which he wants them to make up their own minds, will be delivered with a much quieter outbreathing. It is only when we are doing unaccustomed things with the mind that we have to think consciously about how we fit in our breathing.

It is not only in the activities that I have mentioned that breathing is important. Any period of constructive thinking needs a mind that is not distracted by its physical servant. A few quiet even breaths will put the body into a state of calm inactivity. One should hold the attitude of letting it get on with its own business while you pursue yours undisturbed. We have to accept the dissociation of mind and body at times, because the mind has journeys to make on its own where the body cannot follow. That is our field of adventure, and we shall be freer to explore it if we leave the body behind.

CHAPTER SIX
REPETITION:
AN ACTION TOOL

This is an important 'action tool' at the present time. Because of the inefficient way in which we use our minds, repetition makes up, in some cases, for the lack of energy that we are able to put into our thought. But this will not always be so. When we can consciously direct the energy that is required for our thinking, then repetition will cease to be necessary for any of the circumstances which now demand it.

For such things as learning most physical actions, we have to resort to repetition. This is exampled in such things as playing an instrument, learning how to shuffle a pack of cards, or, more ambitiously, any of the moves made by a card magician which have to be carried out unobserved by his audience. There are many more instances, of course, in which we repeat an action until it can be carried out without our paying any attention to it. During the repetition, the variations that inevitably occur through the lack of muscular coordination, are corrected and gradually eliminated.

Repetition is used to enhance memory of sight and sound, and occasionally of the other products of the senses. To be effective though, it has to be somewhat more than bare physical repetition. In memorizing words, for instance, either the sense of the words or the sound must be included in the repetition. Or in learning to play a difficult phrase on an instrument, or to play a piece by heart, it is important that the mind focuses on the sound each time the phrase is repeated. The repetition will have its effect even if this is not done, because it is the attention of the subconscious mind that is being evoked, so that repetition without concentration on what is being repeated will eventually enable the fingers (or the feet in a dance) to move automatically. It is the autonomic mind that is drilled into giving the muscles the necessary instructions for the movements.

This is a wasteful way of doing anything; wasteful in time and in effort, and there will be a lack of precision in the result. Repetition is a crude tool. It is a kind of sledge-hammer effect which, in the case of making contact with the subconscious mind, is the only method we have at present for attracting its attention. The technique I described in *Mind Your Body* and *A Manual of Self-Healing* relies on repetition to get the message across to the autonomic mind that the body has to do something to repair a defect. This is not too difficult, since the body should have been attending to the matter anyhow, and is not being given something entirely new to perform. That is a conscious and constructive use of repetition. We all know of the reverse, of people who, through constant worry and anxiety have induced ulcers or other bodily ills and defects — psychosomatic illnesses. In the same way that one swallow doesn't make a summer, one anxious thought won't give birth to an ulcer. But if strong emotion is continually pervading the mind, it will seep down into the subconscious and the autonomic mind will react. An energy flow somewhere will become deficient or in excess, and this will result in a corresponding defect appearing in the physical body.

We need to guard our thoughts; we need to learn that all thoughts charged with harmful emotions will have their effect both internally on the body, and externally on their targets. A thought *is* substantial; it is matter, very fine matter, in action. It is not what we take it to be, airy-fairy flickerings of a vapour-like insubstantiality, or just the sensation of chemical changes in the brain, as many scientists would have it. Thought could never have any effect, never achieve anything, if it wasn't material substance of some kind. Energy must have a carrier.

We are simply shutting our eyes and minds if we refuse to accept that thought is matter, matter charged with energy, an energy that we ourselves inject into our thoughts.

By repetition, we continually transmit small parcels of energy with our thought, the build-up of which will eventually have the desired effect. We should, of course — and we will when we have learnt how to release the power of the mind — be able to charge a thought with the necessary amount of energy for the job, and send it on its way. Thought without energy, which ours so often is, is directionless and purposeless, and its form soon fades. For thoughts have forms which, just as the chemical on a photographic plate is capable of reproducing forms 'seen' by a lens of a camera, are capable of being transformed into physical reality.

There are numerous examples of people who have been able to produce on a photographic plate images of which they had thought. A particularly remarkable example of this ability (if one can believe the reports of the many tests that have been made and recorded) is a man called Ted Serios, an American. He was able to reproduce at will pictures from a book he had been looking at previously, when he held an unexposed photographic plate in his hands. The plate was then developed and the picture appeared.

But whether we believe reports such as this or not, we have, sooner or later, to come to grips with the fact that thought is substantial. It is energy-charged, and has effects for good and ill that we do not at present admit, although we can see the result in mass psychology, when crowds are influenced by a dynamic speaker, and we can very often feel the tension in a room as we enter. We can sense a happy atmosphere in a house, or the sinister oppression that pervades a place where cruelty has been committed, or a tragedy has taken place. Perhaps not all of us have this sensitivity, but some of us do, and there are enough to make it clear that here is something unexplained by material science.

When will we wake up to the damage we are doing all the time with thoughts that we believe to be entirely private, and retained within the confines of our skulls? The time cannot be long delayed, because too many things are piling into the unexplained heap; too much is becoming difficult to shrug off, and some scientists are becoming wary of being too didactic about the old assumptions.

Repetition finds a very important place in meditation. Sometimes a mantram is repeated daily for months or even years before its force is able to have an effect on our consciousness. And when using the 'as if' principle (see Chapter 16), constant repetition is necessary before the desired quality has become a natural reaction. All meditation, of the kind that most of us in the Western world are embarking on, relies on repetition for its effectiveness.

Only when we realize the facts about thought which have been staring us in the face for so long, shall we be in a position to learn to develop its full potential. To do so now would be unsafe, more than that, downright dangerous. To have the power, and not to understand what it is capable of doing, would be like teaching a primitive savage how to fire an atomic weapon. Each man has this mind-power within him that could be deadly or bring untold improvement to the circumstances and living conditions of the present age. We are approaching the time when we shall discover how to train for it. Let us hope that, by then, we shall have learnt how to use it aright.

All that is a long way from repetition, but it does explain why repetition is necessary to us now, why we are like an ant examining a micro-circuit and finding it to be just a smooth terrain. We shall not be needing this cumbersome tool much longer; at present it is required as a substitute for inefficient thinking.

CHAPTER SEVEN
SPEECH:
AN ACTION TOOL

It will hardly surprise anybody that I include speech as a tool of the mind. It is, however, such a common, everyday way of bringing the power of the mind into action, that we probably do not think of it quite as a tool. We certainly don't treat it as a tool. And we only occasionally recognize the power that it wields. But a tool it certainly is; sometimes blind and inefficient, the common medium of misunderstanding, sometimes keen and sparkling. It is, of course a secondary tool, depending entirely on thought, however perfunctory it may be, for its effect. Thought is at present largely dependent for the transmission of the energy it wields on the sound of the words and the meaning they convey.

These comprise two distinct elements that go to make up speech; the sounds and the way they are uttered, and the content emanating from the mind. I think many of us do not appreciate how difficult it is to put an idea originating in the mind into the words of our speech. Neither do we pay enough attention to the way in which we manipulate sound, or to the choice of words to express our meaning accurately. Our speech, with few exceptions, is slapdash, imprecise, and badly delivered, and it is habit that has made it so.

To add to all this, there is language, another source of mis-understanding. This is not only the case when one language is being interpreted into another, but also when one is attempting to put into one's own language an idea that is clear in the mind. The limitation of language in this way is not always apparent, but it becomes obvious when one wishes to speak of something of which one's audience has had no previous experience. This may happen because the language does not possess adequate words to express the idea. For instance, translation from Sanskrit, which is a language rich in abstract and philosophical words, into any European language, is a very difficult matter, and frequently a whole phrase will be necessary to translate a single word. Ideas are not readily transformed into words. Speech is not the clear-cut expression of what is in our minds that we think it is.

We are all aware that new sciences, or significant develop-ments of a particular branch of industry, require new words to be invented to enable them to be spoken about. We have the example of 'computer language'. This inadequacy of words is a serious difficulty when one is trying to describe a new aware-ness, because it is usually something of which the listener will not have had previous experience. That is why so much of the mystic literature of past centuries is couched in allegorical terms, for which full understanding can only be gained when a similar expansion of awareness has been experienced.

Nevertheless, speech, at the present time, is very important. We use it badly. We very often do not think carefully before we speak. Just imagine trying to listen to a radio when it has not been properly tuned! That is what we are doing when we speak without having consciously thought of what we are going to say. Idle speech, thoughtless chatter, hasty speech, muddled speech, and many more kinds of speech that we indulge in daily, are all examples of the mishandling of this valuable tool. Self discipline is needed over speech just as much as with other aspects of our behaviour. Rightly used, speech can be enlivening, and inspiring, as we all know when we hear polished speakers like Churchill or Russell, or from today's long list, Enoch Powell, not so much because of what he says but how he says it!

Most of our speech is commonplace in the extreme. We don't

need inspiring subjects in order to speak inspiringly; we need to inject the spark of compulsive listening into ordinary subjects when necessary. Words, in spite of their inability to represent thought accurately, have a very great variety of cadences, can wield delicate differences of urgency, and can exercise calm and comfort to great effect. But the limitation of words and speech is clear. Only when we are able to transmit ideas directly from mind to mind without the intermediary assistance of speech, shall we be able *always* to understand one another with complete clarity. And that time will come — is, in fact, coming already. The evidence of telepathic communication is beginning to impinge on scientific minds. Many tests have been and are being carried out to try to discover the carrier of thought transmission.

We all have this potential, but at present don't need it, and are not imbued sufficiently with love of our fellow men to be trusted with the ability. It is inevitable at present that new discoveries are instantly taken up for harmful purposes. Take, for example, the discovery of the release of atomic power. This, in the years to come, will prove to have been the most significant development in recorded history. It will take time for the adjustment to be made that will remove from it the opprobrium of being a harmful discovery. The invention of the laser is, perhaps, one of the few made recently that found its place in medicine and industry before it was adapted for military use.

Thought transmission is potentially more harmful than atomic power. It would be quite impossible to control. Fortunately, it will come gradually, first of all in those men and women who are sufficiently developed spiritually to use it only for the good of humanity, and a few, as there are at present, who appear to have the gift by chance. Some of the latter will certainly put it to their own selfish purposes.

As the human race begins to learn the message of the 'five commandments' (of The Yoga Sutras of Pantanjali) and leaves the control by the personality behind, so will the ability to transmit and receive thought directly become general. This is not a far fantasy. Telepathic transmission happens now all the time, from humans to animals as well as to each other. But is not under control, is not a conscious action, and is seldom recognized for what it is.

When telepathic communication has become a common ability, speech will naturally play a different role in our everyday life. It will no longer be used for the common interchange of thought that is now so necessary (and often so wasteful and inefficient), for our association with others. The true value of the voice will be its sound, and much about this sound will be discovered and used in healing, and in the control of devices that would otherwise be operated by electricity. Speech will, of course, be used for a long time to come, because differences in the ability to receive clearly and consistently will continue, until the masses have reached the necessary development for mind-to-mind communication to be safe. The situation will be similar to what happens now within a group when one or two people do not speak the common language. The speaker will have to select a language that is common to all. So will he have to use speech when not all of his 'hearers' are able to receive mind-to-mind communication.

But all that is a long way off. What is at hand now for us to work on is the right use of this tool of speech, recognising it as a tool, inadequate though it may be at times, and learning the art of 'right speech'. It is inevitable, and this may be regretted by many, that speech, as it is brought under proper control, will become less frequent. 'Only speak when you have something to say, and when you have thought how to say it,' will be the rule, not to everyone's liking, I know; but as we begin to realise the value of speech and the harm that is done involuntarily through ignorance, by wrong speech, there will be a gradual shift towards regarding speech with the significance it merits, and using it accordingly.

Speech is a valuable tool. We have to develop it by the study of grammar (still very important though decried by many), by reading and the acquisition of vocabulary, and by practice. Learning another language tells us much that we have omitted to learn of our own. Properly used, speech can be dynamic. Words, as sounds, carry energy and this, coupled with the thought energy that accompanies them, can work wonders and leave indelible impressions on the mind. Unfortunately we generate too many unpleasant impressions, harsh and unkind words, fateful words that should never have been uttered, words that let loose war, tyranny, and mass murder; so much speech is fortified with emotional energy that does so much harm. Surely it is time that we recognized the evil of harmful speech and began to cultivate the habit of 'right speech'.

Most of what I have written above is of the harmful aspect of speech. What about its constructive side? What should we do in order to make better use of this tool? First of all we should speak less and with greater care. Much of the harmful speech that occurs today is the result of impulsive or compulsive speech, that is, speech without due thought. We either rattle on, or we burst in with the little bit that we must say before we forget it! Speech is such a valuable tool that it is a crime against common sense to use it improperly. We must begin to regard it in this light. Let us think long enough before speaking to enable us to withold what should not or need not be said. The sort of speech that we so frequently indulge in, with only cursory thought directing the flow of words, and less still that of meaning and significance, should not be allowed. We must become watchers of our speech until it becomes a habit to think first.

In spite of their deficiencies, words are very important, particularly when they are 'wrong' words conveyed with strong emotion. Let us use words as the painter places paint from his brush on the canvas, with the delicate care that will result in the picture he wishes to portray. For it is mind-pictures that we are seeking to transmit by the words we use. If we consider carefully the sort of picture it is, perhaps we would not wish to share it with any one else. We have to develop the kind of mind that will live comfortably with telepathic communication *before* this becomes possible. This can only be done by learning to discriminate between what is fit for general publication and what is not, and disciplining oneself to think only what is. When we are no longer fearful of our secret thoughts becoming public property, then we are ready for telepathic communication. Speech will therefore become an increasingly valuable tool as we learn the art of harmlessness in using it. This, of course, presupposes the harmlessness of thought which engenders it.

CHAPTER EIGHT
ASSOCIATION:
AN ACTION TOOL

This is one of the commonest tools of which we make use. We do so fairly efficiently and mostly subconsciously. We associate both the sound of the spoken word and the sight of the written word with persons, things, and concepts. It is therefore a basic tool for the acquisition and use of knowledge. Without it, memory would be diminished in its cover, and our apprehension of ourselves and of our environment would be much restricted.

I have used this tool deliberately to remember peoples' names, as I am sure many others have. For instance, a man you meet has a rather aquiline bony face. His name is Jones. Jones - bones, and you will never forget it. There is usually something you can pick on to make this association, their dress, actions, or speech, or perhaps even the circumstances in which you met. Some people remember names naturally; I don't, and I frequently have to have recourse to this dodge.

When I was a boy, there was a game called 'Kim's game' which was popular at parties given for young people. It was, of course, Kipling's Kim who gave it his name. A number of articles are exhibited on a tray for a period of a minute or so; the tray is then removed from sight. One then has to write down as many of the articles as one can remember. At that time, I was a keen student of magic and conjuring (there is a difference), and I had learnt a memory trick that worked in this way. One first memorized a number of mind pictures, the kind of empty picture into which an article could conspicuously be introduced. Such would be a football field, a lake, skating rink etc. It is only necessary to visualize momentarily each article in one of these empty pictures without trying in any way to remember it. Later, on recalling the picture, the article stands out clearly. Let us try an example. Suppose the picture is of a church and the article a frying pan. Mentally picture the parson in the pulpit emphasizing some point in his sermon by waving the frying pan at his congregation. You don't have to try to remember the picture, it will leap to your mind as soon as you recall the picture of the church. There, at once, you see the eccentric parson with his frying pan!

This principle was made into a memory trick by attaching to each of say, twenty pictures of this kind, a number from one to twenty. A list of articles is made by the audience, each numbered from one to twenty. This list is read out to the performer, and when this has been done, he asks anyone to call out a number. He is able to name immediately the article at that number in the list. I elaborated this trick to turn it into a really remarkable feat of memory, that of remembering a whole pack of cards which had been dealt face up once before the performer. For this I had prepared fifty-two numbered empty pictures, each corresponding to a position in the pack. Each card itself was represented by an article carefully chosen so that it was suitable to be inserted mentally into any of the empty pictures. For instance, the three of hearts was a hammer, the three of clubs, a comb, the seven of diamonds, a top hat, the ace of spades, a spade etc. It took some time to learn these one hundred and four correspondences, but once done, it was only necessary to fit the image corresponding to the card into the picture corresponding to the number at which it was dealt. When I became proficient at this, it was possible for me to have the pack dealt face down into any number of packets and then to name any card lying at any position in any packet. For instance, if I were asked for the fourth card down in the fifth packet out of seven, a quick calculation would tell me that it was the thirty-fifth card dealt and this I could discover by referring to the picture corresponding to that number.

I have described this 'memory trick' in detail because it does illustrate a quite remarkable use of this tool of association, one not, perhaps, of very much use except for remembering shopping lists! The combination of the two pictures will remain clear in the memory for a long time, sometimes for many days or until others are substituted for it. If I ask you now what it was that I put into the picture of the church, you will have no difficulty in replying without having to think. Some people have the gift of making use of association quite subconsciously and through it develop remarkable memories.

In using the creative imagination (see Chapter 16) we also use the tool of association. By associating positively in our imagination the quality we wish to associate with our general behaviour, as though we already had it, we trigger off its creation. Then by using the tool of repetition, this spark of creation is fanned, and gradually we find that we are acquiring the quality we set out to develop. It is the association with oneself of the product of the creative imagination, that brings it to birth in the conscious behaviour of the individual.

If this sounds too improbable to some of my readers, I suggest they try it out on some minor trait of character that they would like to have. In doing so, they will have to use the tool of mind-picturing, seeing themselves actually behaving as they would like to, and avoiding the sort of thinking attitude and behaviour they wish to eliminate.

Association is not all good, of course; it can either demean or exalt depending on with what or whom one is associating. The Buddha enjoined his hearers to keep company with good men. The effects of association, good and bad, are common in today's society. They always have been so, but today, perhaps, the extremes are more apparent, and more accessible.

Unlike many of the tools that I am writing about, association is a method of using the mind that we are all aware of. We could make more use of it to our benefit. I am not suggesting that everyone should go round with lists of pictures in his head waiting to fit others into them, but the principle of association should be kept in mind, and used in the many cases where it is applicable. I have included it here because of its two very important uses, for memory and for character forming by combining it with the creative imagination. If there is a simple way of doing a thing then, as a spin-off from Ockham's Razor,* it should be used in preference to others.

In the business of raising the threshold of awareness of the mind, we shall find ourselves relying on this tool more and more. That is if we are pursuing the path to the higher mind consciously. It is therefore necessary for us to recognize it for what it is, a very important partner of the creative imagination.

I do not need to say any more about this tool of association except to emphasize that it *is* a tool and should be brought into use when the conditions so indicate.

*Note: Ockham was a Franciscan philosopher who lived in the fourteenth century. He dissected every question as with a razor. The term Ockham's Razor refers to the process of analyzing and eliminating all unnecessary facts or constituents of a subject under scrutiny.

CHAPTER NINE
DISCRIMINATION:
A SETTING-UP TOOL

One of the disadvantages in the way in which we use our minds at present, is that we nearly always have too much thought trying to occupy our attention. Much, if not most of this, is unwanted. It is in discriminating against those thoughts that are not germane to the thinking being undertaken, that the tool of discrimination comes into play. I have dealt earlier with the elimination of those intruding thoughts which interrupt our concentration; the function of discrimination is somewhat different. We always have to decide which of the many thoughts we may have about a subject are really relevant and which are not, and this is not as simple as it sounds because, unless we keep our objective clearly in mind, we lose the basis for our discrimination. For grand designs, we have to do this in the planning stage, for example the general preparing for a battle, or the Prime Minister setting out the objectives of the current parliamentary session, but we do not generally feel that this kind of attention is necessary before we embark on those thinking projects with which we are continually occupied. One of the principles that should be adhered to in mental work, as it usually is in all physical undertakings, is that of economy of effort. One has only a certain amount of force or energy available for a given project; it should not, therefore, be wasted.

A good example of this art of discrimination is seen in the way an expert chairman will prepare himself for a meeting. He goes through all the items on the agenda, considering all the probable opposition that will be raised against each point, and decides how it should be countered. He marks, in his mind, certain red herrings or non-relevant views that are likely to be pressed, and decides how these should be disposed of. A good chairman, if he has done his homework, will have a fair idea of how the meeting is going to turn out, and may even make a rough draft of the decisions he feels will be arrived at before he goes to the meeting. A man who can conduct a meeting like this has used great discrimination in sorting out the important points, discarding irrelevancies, and generally bringing a neat packet of thinking to the meeting, that will be clear, precise, to the point, and convincing.

That is an example of the sort of discrimination that should be used in tackling all the problems that meet us every day. The actions of mental sorting and filtering the mass of information that usually flits around in our minds, make sure that we bring to the consideration of the problem only those facts, views, and proposals that really concern it, and will affect the outcome. This ensures that whatever mental energy we can make available will be used with the greatest effect. Thought penetrates a problem just as a drill penetrates metal. The success of the penetration depends on the energy that can be applied to it; this, after all, is common sense.

There is another use for discrimination, that we become aware of when we are seeking to increase the levels of awareness on which our minds make contact with reality. Up to now, for most of us, reality is what is embraced by the range of our physical senses, and what can be deduced from this field of contact. But we must not assume that this constitutes the total potential of the reach of our minds. Most certainly it does not. The mind is able to make contacts well above the frequency range of physical matter. We have seen or read of many people who have gifts of clairvoyance, clairaudience, telepathy, or ability to see the aura which surrounds the physical body of a living being. Many people tend to treat reports of these sensitivities with scepsis or downright disbelief. This is not surprising. When something is said to exist that we are unable to fit into the possible, according to our philosophy, and of which we have had no experience, then, rather than have this uncomfortable cuckoo nagging continually at our conception of the possible, it is better to shut it out by putting it into the category of 'not to be believed'. But if one allows oneself a reasonable flexibility, there is too much evidence to discount altogether the possibility that there are those who can see non-physical substance.

If our convictions allow us to accept such goings-on for the purpose of taking a new look at our concept of reality, then we have to use the tool of discrimination in a new way. It is not now a case of relevant facts and information, it is a case of 'is it possible that this is a part of the reality that lies beyond the detection limits of my physical senses — at present?' We have to learn anew to discriminate the real from the unreal. And, in this connection, we have been presented with a nice paradox by the scientists, who explain that the matter we regard as forming the solidity of our world, is in reality composed of atoms and all the bustling activity that exists within them. This is quite beyond the range of our physical senses to confirm, and yet we have accepted it as a reality that lies behind all the various forms that make up our physical world. This is so different from the reality reported to us by our senses, that we tend to create in our minds two separate worlds, one as given by the senses, and the other as revealed by the instruments of the scientists. We now have to look further than science is willing at present to penetrate. By using the mind, we have to find new criteria of reality, stepping firmly behind or above the barrier erected by our senses. At first this is difficult, but as one begins to map the way, the habit of looking inwards becomes established.

There are always overriding considerations that we have to keep in mind in order to test any new vision of reality — does this new vision lead me to a broader, more inclusive view of humanity, the purpose of our evolution and my place in it? Following on from this, of course, there are all sorts of subsidiary questions that one can make use of in the process of discrimination. How would it affect my relations with my fellow men? Would it encourage me to put more emphasis on the requirements and comforts of the personality–self, or would it lead me to feel the needs of others as more important than my own? There are many such awkward questions that one can ask in order to establish whether what has entered the mind is from soul, the essence of the human being, or from an intellectual presentation of how the personality should act. A change in the understanding of the reality of the human being that stands behind his physical form, will bring a corresponding change in our interpretation of the world in which we live and move, and have our being, an interpretation for which we have, at present, very limited means. It is by using the tool of discrimination that we have the potential of expanding these means, a discrimination that must be applied to all new offerings of thought and belief, from wherever they may come.

Discrimination is a tool that needs to be honed to an ever increasingly fine edge, in order to detect the subtle distinctions with which one will be faced. As with the use of all tools, 'practice makes perfect', and the more we consciously use this tool for the purpose of discriminating between what is real in our lives and what is not, the more indispensable will it become in the process of discovering the true nature of our being and the purpose for which we exist.

More and more as the mind reaches into higher awarenesses, will the tool of discrimination be used to discard all those thoughts that belong to earlier patterns of understanding. Many of these will become automatic in the process of gradually relegating intellectual activity to the role of the subconscious. If we are to be active in the realms of higher thought, we must not be held back by what will have become purely utilitarian thinking for the benefit of the body and its physical needs.

One way of ensuring this has been the custom in the east for centuries. A man wishing to pursue the search for illumination would isolate himself and live a life of concentrated meditation, with the minimum attention to the needs of the body that are required to sustain life. But this kind of action is not necessary and, in any case, it is not possible for one who lives in the west. It is, after all, mind control and discrimination that decide the priorities of one's existence; it is not the actions themselves that determine where these lie, but the significance that is attached to them. Granted, it is more difficult in the hustle and bustle of a businessman's life to make progress in his search for higher understanding, but, in the present stage of mental development (in which a boundary is about to be crossed), it is possible. It will be found that, once a conscious connection has been made with higher mind, in a miraculous way it will lead to opportunities and contacts that will greatly encourage the searcher and facilitate his task.

In the discrimination that will then be necessary, there will be two pulls, one from the burgeoning higher mind and the other from the personality. That is why I said that it is necessary to keep in mind constantly the task on which one has embarked. The pull of the personality is strong, and at first continual, and it has the force of common sense acting for the good of the individual. In fact, the requirements of the personality will be met by the higher mind without the individual's attention, but only the necessary ones, not those which give preference to the personality over the higher nature. In this stage of the opening up of the higher mind, discrimination is difficult, but the more the 'I' becomes representative of the higher nature and not of the personality, the more will the necessary discrimination become a natural response.

CHAPTER TEN
THE SUBCONSCIOUS:
AN ACTION TOOL

The subconscious consists of a number of different functions of mind, some of which we know about, such as the autonomic mind. This takes care of all those activities of the body that continue without any attention from the conscious mind; it attends to the maintenance and repair of the body as far as this is possible. In addition to this very important function there are, however, other mind activities and potentials, some of which the psychologists manipulate and explain, but unfortunately with a jargon that many find difficult to follow. There is little doubt that racial and other memories still exist in this region of the mind, and almost certainly influence the conscious mind without our knowing anything about it. We know that what we might not take in consciously when listening to a speaker, or looking idly at a moving scene, is received and retained by the subconscious. The subliminal impression is a good example of how far this ability extends. A picture flashed before the eyes too fast for the conscious mind to interpret, is nevertheless fully understood and retained by the subconscious.

I do not want to enlarge on the position that the subconscious holds in our mental activities. What I have written above is

simply intended to show that a part of the mind is always active
below the level of consciousness. This continual activity can be
put to good use provided we use the right technique which, as a
tool of the mind, it requires.

A very important way in which it can be relied upon to come
to the assistance of the conscious mind is in the sifting of new
knowledge or information, and then serving up to the conscious
mind what can be accepted with confidence, and what must be
rejected. This may take time. In the case of new directions of
thinking which will affect one's whole attitude to life and
relations with others, it could be months or even years before
certainty suddenly appears in the mind. In such a case, it is
probable that the information being sifted is significant enough
to bring about a change in the basis of one's belief. This inflow of
confirming thought leaves no room for doubt. One simply
knows that this is what one has to believe. During the dead
period, all the pros and cons, the rationalities and incon-
sistencies, have been examined by the subconscious, and shape
given to the final pattern of thought that it knows will be
accepted by its conscious counterpart.

I always use this method. I never attempt to argue the toss and
try to find out whether I should believe this or that, or what
logical, rational, or experiental grounds there might be for either
believing or not believing. One has to prepare thoroughly the
material to be sent down to the subconscious. This alone is an
exercise in sizing up the pros and cons. The conscious mind must
review the whole proposal that one is being asked to accept.
Spend some time positively thinking of, but not judging, all the
new information you have been given as teaching, or through
what you have read; some new theory of existence, perhaps, or
desirable behaviour, or of our relationship to the rest of
creation, animal vegetable and mineral, as well as human. It is
only seldom that one is able to reply or react by saying or
thinking yes, that is how it is'. Sometimes, indeed, this does
happen; it seems as though one's mental eyes have been
suddenly opened so that the reaction is 'why the devil didn't I see
that before', but that is a rare occurrence.

There comes a time in each person's life when he or she is
ready for the next widening of knowledge, and I am not
referring to the increasing complexities and technicalities of the

many specializations of our industrial age, but what is referred to as the expansion of consciousness. This leads thinking on to a higher plane, so that one begins to be aware of contacts and sources of knowledge that previously were beyond the reach of one's mind. It is at just such a time that, bewildered by what one has discovered or heard, the technique of letting the sub-conscious do the work of unscrambling all the new thoughts jostling for place in the forefront of one's thinking, should be employed. The subconscious should be given a free rein to mull over what has been sent down, and then serve up an acceptable frame of thinking, which will allow one to continue smoothly with daily life, perhaps changed in direction, but confidently 'on course'.

If it is the kind of sorting out that requires many years — as I found when digesting the Buddhist Mahayana concept of the 'void' — it will be found that all the time one's thinking *is* changing, but imperceptably, and it will not be until later that one will understand what has been going on. This method of 'subconsciousing' prevents one 'jumping the gun' and accepting something that one is not yet ready for, that is, when proper understanding is not possible. This, which so often happens, can lead to fanaticism or alternatively to a repressed irritant that will hinder the proper development of one's thinking. The purpose of these acquisitions of new knowledge or new awareness, is to channel the way to higher mind where conscious contact with the essence or soul of the individual can be made. The realization that there has been a change, usually comes suddenly. The understanding of this or that is more confident; some view that has become outworn is found to have been dropped altogether from the accepted pattern of belief; the new understanding that has taken its place seems like an old friend, so readily acceptable is it.

If the sorting-out is assisted by a conscious reaching out towards the higher mind, then the result will come much more quickly, in a matter of weeks or, at the most, months. One should resist the temptation to return impatiently in thought to the 'teaching' or the new presentation of knowledge during the period of digestion. This will only interfere with the orderly method of examination that the subconscious adopts. One has to be patient; suddenly perhaps, but not necessarily, in a flash, the form of truth to be accepted will be there in the mind. It will come with complete confidence that this *is* the truth to be accepted, and that it will lead to the next expansion of consciousness that lies on the path ahead.

This flash of revelation can be experienced in a much more mundane manner, one which is adopted by many businessmen and others with technical, managerial and procedural problems. I have a friend who is a brilliant engineer with an exceptional ability of visualization, particularly where complicated machines or instruments are concerned. He always treats problems in the way I describe below.

Before going to sleep at night, he goes through all the information that he has collected about the problem, noting the pros and cons of possible solutions, but not attempting to give them any precedence. When he has gone over the whole matter, he dismisses it from his mind and gives a conscious direction to the subconscious to work on it. If you follow this routine, then either when you wake up in the morning, or suddenly during the day when you are busily occupied with something else, the solution will be presented to you in a flash. You will probably react with some such thought as 'so that's how I do it'.

This practice of subconsciousing has other uses. As one gets older, the short term memory tends to become unreliable. This worries many people, really worries them, and they begin to think that they are losing the use of their minds. I have described in Chapter 12 how to put this difficulty into the hands of the subconscious. It will seldom fail to come up with the answer. But one must resist the temptation to return time after time to see whether the missing item can be recalled. The subconscious mind seems to work best in this kind of function when the conscious mind is occupied and therefore not trying to interfere. I suggest that any reader who has this difficulty should try out this routine. You may not be successful the first couple of times (don't forget that expectation and confidence which are tools of the mind are relevant in most of its uses), but the subconscious *will* take the hint, it will look up the forgotten fact in its memory bank, and deliver up the answer to your conscious mind.

The subconscious is used very much like a mental dustbin, collecting all the garbage from the mind that is not wanted at the moment, is too dangerous to retain in consciousness, or simply has no function or place in one's thinking. It is a great step forward to be able to make use of it in the constructive way described in this chapter, as many already do. It is a very useful tool. One should build up a constructive liaison with one's sub-conscious so that it will become a helper in the business of living, and not the unintentional menace that it so often is. I believe that this way of making a responsive contact with the subconscious will open up all sorts of other ways in which the subconscious can be given the opportunity of co-operating with the conscious, and that the familiarity thus developed may result in the repressions that build up dangerous pressures in the subconscious being less likely to appear.

CHAPTER ELEVEN
THE ACCESSORIES:
ACTION TOOLS

I now come to a group of tools that are in fairly common use; many of them are held to be mumbo-jumbo, superstition, or just plain nonsense. I am referring to all those things that are used to acquire information that cannot be obtained through the senses alone or through scientific methods. Such are the pendulum, radionics, the crystal ball, the I Ching, and many forms of fortune telling. In my opinion, the first and foremost of these is the pendulum. My reason for giving it this dominant position is because, not only can one locate water, minerals, and lost or hidden property with the pendulum, but it is able to provide information about historical and archeological sites, and events that took place there. It is also used widely for diagnosing physical ills. In fact, there seems to be no limit to the kind of information the pendulum can reveal, if the person using it is able to put his mind in a relaxed and receptive mood and ask the right questions. There is no magic about this. The pendulum does not move on its own. It is moved subconsciously by the muscles of the fingers and wrist.

What I have said in Chapter 18 is that pure mind, that is mind not obstructed and limited by the physical medium the brain through which it operates, has access to all knowledge. But it has no means of bringing this knowledge to the notice of the conscious mind and thence to the brain, because the attention of consciousness is directed to the stimuli it receives from the physical body, or through its agencies. It is just beginning to be occupied with the functioning of the higher mind, but this is mainly along lines that have originated through physical contacts. Pure mind is not yet able to reach consciousness without becoming contaminated. Until we are able to subdue the workings of the lower mind and tune in to the intuition without obstruction from the habitual activity of our physically orientated consciousness, we shall not be able to avail ourselves of the unlimited store of knowledge that is the intuition's field.

To understand the role of the various accessories that I shall discuss in this chapter, we have to accept that the mind has access to a great store of knowledge that we have not yet developed the ability to bring down into consciousness. It is the intuitional part of the mind that embraces this knowledge, but it functions above the level of consciousness at which we are at present polarized, just as the autonomic mind operates below it. The one is superconscious, the other subconscious.

The operator of the pendulum asks a question mentally that can be answered by 'yes' or 'no'. These answers are usually given by a clockwise or anticlockwise swing of the pendulum. There is quite an art in the mental attitude behind these questions; any preconceived idea or desire for the answer to fit some pet theory must be excluded. Tom Graves, in his book *Dowsing: Techniques and Applications*, (Turnstone Press, 1976), gives an interesting example of the sort of question that has to be asked. When dowsing on an archeological site, if the dowser fixes his mind on a particular date, the pendulum will reveal only those artifacts that date from that period.

What must happen is that the superconscious part of the mind is able to communicate with the subconscious autonomic mind, which in turn directs the muscles of the wrist and fingers to move in such a way as to initiate a swing in one direction or the other. But the conscious mind can also give instructions to these muscles, and will do so if the mental attitude is not held clear of all bias for a particular answer. I know that those who operate the pendulum for medical analysis have to be careful that they do not hold any kind of conclusion as to what the cause of the trouble might be because, if they do, that is what the pendulum will reveal! A certain very successful healer who uses the pendulum for his diagnoses, told me that, when in any doubt as to his mind being completely unbiased, he asks other members of his healing team to check his finding. The mind, when working with the pendulum, must be in a completely relaxed and receptive state, so that it cannot interfere with the communication between the higher mind and the subconscious.

At first sight, it is strange that there should be this communication between the intuitional and the autonomic parts of the mind short-circuiting consciousness. We forget how busy and distracted the conscious mind usually is in its function of dealing with stimuli, messages, and their associations, in their continual and myriad variations. While its reach is gradually being extended from the limitations of the rational concrete mind to the higher mind, we have, as yet, only experienced the fringe of mental activity that this part of the mind will generate. The autonomic mind, on the other hand, though busy, is concerned with routine and very limited activity in comparison with the conscious mind. It therefore is able to react, and does so in many different ways, to contact coming from the intuitional mind. It is an indication, perhaps, of the positive approach being made by the higher mind at this stage of man's development.

Whether the question has to be passed from the conscious to the superconscious is anyone's guess, but it would seem more probable that the subconscious acts as an intermediary in this case. Otherwise, it would be possible for the superconscious to pass the answer directly to the conscious mind in the way in which the intuition occasionally works at present, and will increasingly do in the years to come. Whichever it is, the mental attitude in which the question is 'put' is critical. The question has to be received by the subconscious in clear terms, and there are only two ways in which this can be done. The first is by repetition (the way used in the healing technique described in *A Manual of Self-Healing*), and the other by a sharp intense concentration on the question, that keeps out all influences that the conscious mind would like to exert. The most successful operators of the pendulum technique are those who have developed (or perhaps already possessed) the ability for the quiet receptive kind of concentration and can switch this from one question to another with ease.

This is the basic explanation of all the various accessories that people use to penetrate the present, the past, and sometimes the future, with varying degrees of success. As the mind gradually learns to make contact with the higher mind, and therefore brings the intuition into regular use, these accessories will be regarded as clumsy and unnecessary. This is evidenced by what is happening in the next class of accessory I shall discuss, where complicated instruments are, in many cases, being replaced by graphs and even pure mental reactions.

There are many theories offered for the way in which these accessories work, and, although many consider that their working is largely a matter of chance expectation, a sincere evaluation of the results would have to come to the conclusion that 'there is something in it'. We are entering the age of the discovery of 'energy'. And I mean that, not in the scientific sense, but rather in the esoteric sense, that behind all phenomena lie energies of a very great variety. It is only recently that we have been forced to believe in the powerful energy that lies behind what we cannot see or sense in any way. We have been introduced, for example, to X-rays, to infra-red and infra-violet, to radio waves, to sound waves, gamma waves, and many others. The ordinary person's world is to such an extent being filled with invisible energies, that the first explanation for some unexplained phenomena is likely to be that some unknown energy is at work. Strangely enough, the one energy we do not consider is the energy of thought, but we have arrived at a situation where we are going to have to. I shall be discussing this in a later chapter; here I would only like to point out that the energy of thought is using accessories to overcome the lack of understanding we are demonstrating about the nature of thought and its connection with energy.

Dowsing
It is the wide spectrum that is covered by the pendulum operators from water divining to questions like 'Was King Arthur buried here?', that makes them so interesting. The experienced operators, through patiently gathered experience, have developed a technique that extends the versatility of the

pendulum. They have discovered that different lengths of the cord by which the pendulum is suspended indicate specific relationships to materials, dates, and even abstract ideas. These lengths can be found in books on working with a pendulum, but a great deal of practice is necessary before the beginner can make practical use of this kind of refinement. Another reason for putting the pendulum first among the various accessories used as tools of the mind, is that it has been accepted as a legitimate way of locating water underground and of prospecting for minerals either from a map or on site. There can be no doubt that something makes the diviner's twig 'twitch' and the pendulum rotate. The suggestion that energy coming from the water or the minerals is responsible for the movement, evades the question as to why this should happen only when the operator asks a certain mental question. Perhaps it is somewhat disillusioning to learn that the agents responsible for the movement are one's own muscles! That maybe, but it is a stimulating and challenging thought that the information and the directions to the muscles is coming from one's own mind. There are many, of course, who believe the whole story to be nonsense, but it is hardly possible that they have taken the trouble to study all the evidence that has accumulated over the centuries and is available in many books, before reaching such a conclusion.

Radionics

The next accessory I want to consider is certainly less acceptable to the scientific mind than dowsing, but there are many practitioners who have considerable evidence of successful healing achieved by radionic treatment for humans, animals, and plants. There is also however, equal evidence to show that a great many treatments fail to have any effect. This may be due either to the uncertainty, which must always be present with any method of healing, or it may be that the 'boxes' presumed to be radiating the energy necessary for healing are not as effective as they are held to be by the radionic practitioners.

In radionic analysis, whatever is used, whether it be the 'black box', a chart, or other medium, is another way of bypassing the conscious mind. When using the box, the diagnosis of the part of the body affected and a definition of the trouble, are given by the phenomenon of a 'stick' when the finger is rubbed lightly on a rubber strip, and the instrument is 'tuned' to a particular frequency. The stumbling block to understanding this is that there is no electricity powering the instrument. It is an energy unknown to science or to anyone else, and is not accepted as existing. Nevertheless, most remarkable results have been obtained with animal patients, plants and crops as well as human beings.

The instrument, with its dials for tuning is obviously not necessary for obtaining an analysis, for many practitioners now use a chart in conjunction with a pendulum. But they still rely on the box of dials and coils to transmit the healing energy to the patient. This is where no satisfactory explanation as to how the object is achieved has been suggested. What is the initiator of this energy? Once the piece of hair, blood spot, or a photograph of the patient has been put in the special receptacle in order to make the connection with the patient, the box is left to its own devices, and the practitioner's mind is free to attend to something else. For the box to be able to continue to transmit healing energy, there must be some other source of energy that is directed by the setting of the dials on the instrument. This, in my opinion, must be considered to lie outside the purview of mind.

There are two clear principles employed in the radionic technique. First, the tapping of the intuitional mind to obtain information about the patient's condition, and secondly, the direction of energy of some kind to the patient to effect a cure. If one accepts that there is something behind the technique of radionics, and I think one must, it would seem that the whole array of dials and coils is unnecessary — certainly for obtaining the required information, and probably for the transmission of the healing energy as well. In time, when the energy is identified, it will probably be possible to transmit it by mind alone. At present, in analysis, it is just another way of bypassing the conscious mind, but instead of the autonomic mind directing the muscles of the wrist and fingers, it affects the skin of the rubbing finger to bring about a 'stick'.

What exercises my mind is the use of the box for transmitting the healing energy, because I doubt whether healing energy of any sort, and I include electricity, heat etc., can be fully effective unless mind direction is concerned in its application. With healers, as opposed to conventional medicine, this sometimes takes the form of physical energy — so-called prana — being consciously directed into the patient's body. In other cases, the healer opens himself as a channel for energy to pass through him to the patient. And what is called spiritual healing is a form of power being channelled through the healer producing immediate change in the diseased or defective part of the body. All of these require the continued conscious attention of the healer. The healing energy of the box appears to be divorced from a healer's mind, and therefore it is a radically different situation. Perhaps more success with radionic treatment would be achieved if the box were daily 'recharged' by the practitioner directing energy from his mind to the patient via the box.

It seems clear from both of the accessories I have discussed, that the higher mind is trying to break through the barrier put up by the conscious mind, with its attention riveted on the physical world and the constant messages received from the senses. We can see many instances where this is happening, and the use of the accessories is an interesting example of an alternative route to initiating physical reactions. These reactions may, of course, be of sight, hearing, touch, scent, or taste. But some of these are less likely to be used than others. The first two I have discussed both use the sense of touch, and it is the muscles that are doing the work of the seer.

The next group of accessories I want to consider is that which comprises all forms of fortune telling with cards, crystal ball, the I Ching sticks etc. Some of these barely come into the category of mental tools, but they are believed in by many, and should be looked at. There are many, too, who regard the whole gamut of psychic forecasts as codswallop and, on the evidence, they have reason for this view. I don't want to embark on a discussion as to whether these devices have any proven success beyond chance; that must be a conclusion that comes from experience, or from information from others which can be confirmed in some way. What I do want to indicate is that *if* there is substance in the claims of those operating these various accessories, then they are being used in exactly the same way as the pendulum and the black box. They somehow allow the conscious mind to be bypassed and knowledge from the intuitional level of mind to produce a reaction in some way or other. In the cases of the devices mentioned above, the reaction is mainly on the psychic senses, which, in most of us, are not under the control of the conscious mind.

Astrology
I haven't included astrology in the fortune-telling devices already mentioned because I consider that it is in a class of its own. Present day astrology as popularly presented in most of our daily papers is mumbo-jumbo of the crudest sort, but astrology *per se* is, or should be, an exact science. Unfortunately, we do not, at present, know enough about the various energies entering our world and affecting everything in it. When these energies have been identified, their varying effects on physical emotional and mental matter studied and understood, then astrology will step out of the realm of fancy and become a serious interpreter of known factual occurrences.

Crystal Gazing
The case of crystal gazing too, is a special one. Here, the crystal ball is used as an intermediary in which the psychic sense of sight is encouraged to bypass the conscious mind. The visions which the fortune teller sees are, of course, in his mind and, if they do not step simply from the imagination, may have originated in the intuitional mind. The psychic senses in most of us need some stimulus before they can function; frequently this is provided by a strong emotion, and apparently concentrating on the crystal ball can do this too. It cannot be very reliable because the imagination can so easily interfere.

Cards and I Ching
With playing cards and the I Ching sticks, it is doubtful whether the intuitional mind comes into the picture, rather it is probably a rousing of the psychic sense, and in one where this is not under control the results must be very unreliable. Nevertheless, in both these systems of forecasting, as with the others I have discussed, it is clear that knowledge not normally available to the conscious mind is being obtained via another route.

It is because we are in the slow process of developing direct contact with the higher, the intuitional mind, that part of the mind through which the true 'resident', the soul, expresses itself, that these strange tools have been found to evade some of the obstacles that are presently preventing that contact being established.

The reason why I have called these tools accessories, is because they will be abandoned in due course, as the mind develops the ability to make direct contact with the intuitional mind without their aid. This development can be hastened by special meditation practice, and many thousands have started to do this.

CHAPTER TWELVE
MEMORY:
AN ACTION TOOL

Memory is such an obvious tool of the mind that there is little that need be said about it. It is the ability to store information below the level of consciousness and to recover it selectively at will. Today we have the parallel of this in the memory bank of a computer; but unlike the computer we have different grades of memory, short term, long term, and another range of information that we might call deep memory. This last kind of memory is held securely behind a barrier which prevents it from surfacing into consciousness except on rare occasions. Deep memory is of interest, firstly because we know little about it, and secondly because of the extraordinary amount of information that it contains. It is here that memory of the past takes us back into the womb and to existence in previous lives. Some of this information has been recovered by hypnosis. Of course, it is difficult to prove that it is, in fact, memory that has been released, but there has been much circumstantial evidence produced through historical research in locations where a previous life is said to have been lived. One might ask 'why should these memories not be available to all and at will?' A few moments thought would provide a commonsense answer:

'because of the sufferings and horrors that have ended many lives, and the effect these would have on the present life if they were continually in consciousness.' This deep memory contains also what the psychologists, I believe, call 'racial memory', that is memories that are common to all and which stem from the evolution of the human being from his primitive ancestors.

As a tool of the mind, memory exists in order to relieve the pressure on the conscious mind, and leave it free to handle the matters that concern the activities of the human being and his contacts with the outside world. This is a very convenient arrangement and although we have, at present, only partial control of this faculty, it serves us well. As one grows older, there is a noticeable falling off in the short term memory, and frequently there is a much more vivid recovery of long term events. The nuisance of a failing memory can be lessened by imitating the procedure employed with a computer, that of 'pressing the recall button'. If one has forgotten something that it is particularly necessary to recall, the trick is to put a suitable question mentally, and follow this by saying mentally 'press the recall button', with the meaning that you are instructing the subconscious to send up the answer. In most cases, the answer will come up within a short time; sometimes it may not be until later in the day, but it will come. I think that there is no doubt that, in time, we shall be able in much the same way, to retrieve the memory of the more distant events contained within our deep memory. The whole function of memory is to provide us with experience without clogging the normal working of the conscious mind. When we have the ability to tap the deep memory, we shall have available to us a much greater store of experience, which, at present, only makes itself felt through the subconscious, and that usually with harmful results. In the same way that the psychiatrist is able to release the pressure built up in the subconscious by a repressed thought which may, at the time, have been too disturbing to retain in consciousness, so shall we, by bringing a distant memory to the surface of consciousness at will and fully under control, be able to relieve a symptom in our body or behaviour for which the distant memory had been responsible.

When we have developed the ability to call on the deep memory at will, we shall have increased very greatly the value of this tool of the mind as a store of memories from which we can draw, and which we can make use of to add to our experience. There are many who have the ability of recovering memories of previous lives, but it is not usually fully under their control. The books of Arthur Guirdham tell of the cases of several people who have reincarnated together since Roman times. They all remember details of previous lives in the early nineteenth, the thirteenth, and the seventh centuries, as well as in Roman times. Their memories tally in a remarkable manner, and the telling of their story is most convincing. If this ability is not under control, it can be dangerous. It should be possible to send the thought back to the deep memory pool and thus prevent what might otherwise become a nagging presence, with all the trouble that could cause. We have enough trouble from thoughts representing immediate memory that we cannot dismiss; to add to these all those from which we are at present mercifully protected would increase our load of worries.

I believe, but without any scientific or medical evidence, that the break in our memory, which exists between the deep memory and our conscious thinking, is a break or a barrier that is to be found in the brain. It is only on coming into incarnation that the danger from harmful deep memories looms, because, if they seep into the subconscious, which they sometimes do, they have the same results as the repressed thoughts dealt with by the psychiatrist. Without a physical body, we can accept these memories without fear, and recall and dismiss them just as we now do the thousands of memories that colour our minds each day of our lives. In the bodiless state there is no subconscious where suppressed thoughts can smoulder and send their harmful energy to the brain, for there is no brain either.

This brain 'curtain' is part of our physical inheritance, and will remain so until such time as we have gained total control over memory recall, so that no thought will be allowed to remain in the subconscious with its destructive pressure intact. We shall then be able to realize our potential of a far wider memory control than we have at present, one that will go beyond the limit set by our own personal experience through, maybe, thousands of lives. But this is a faculty that we shall not acquire until we have made considerable progress towards becoming a spiritual being as opposed to mainly a material one.

Tudor Pole, in his books, refers frequently to this ability to tune into records covering events since evolution began, and he describes the difficulty that this entails. Although he is gifted in this way, his disinclincation to make use of the ability is evident.

Memory varies greatly in different individuals, but we can all improve our memories by training and by the proper co-operation with the other tools of the mind such as repetition, association, mind-picturing, concentration, etc. All these, most of which we already understand as aids to memory, are tools of the mind which, when used in conjunction with memory, will enhance the accuracy of recall. At present, the unreliability of recall is brought about by the lack of energy with which the thought is clothed before it is sent down for storage. In the distant future, when intellectual thinking has sunk below the threshold of consciousness, as the autonomic mind has, memory will be complete and entirely automatic, as it very occasionally is now.

Although medical science at present states that memory is related directly to electrical circuits set up in the brain (or if not circuits, then electrical potentials), and has demonstrated that memory of an event can be brought into conscious perception if certain areas of the head are contacted by electrodes, this does not seem to me to explain the working of memory. It is only a secondary effect. True, first effect memory resides in the mind. It is the mind that forms the electrical potentials in the brain, for the specific purpose of making the recall of the memories of this earthly life easier. It is, of course, important that deep memory, going back before the present incarnation, should not be stored in this way. It must be stored in some way in the mind. As the esotericist believes, it is stored between lives in a 'mental unit' and retained in succeeding incarnations as deep memory in the mind but not, at present, accessible to the brain. It is a much more impenetrable barrier than that between the conscious and subconscious. At the present time it is only penetrated by a few rare individuals.

Any memory resulting from events and experience in the present life, if it is to be recalled with the physical sensations that accompanied them, must have some corresponding connection with the brain, where these sensations are registered and recorded. This connection is formed by the discrete circuits or potentials set up with the original event. What I am saying is that it is primarily in the mind that memory resides, and in the mind all memories have equal status. It is only when the mind enters incarnation that two classes of memory are set up — recallable and non-recallable. All new memories forge more or less permanent connections with the brain, while the old memories become inaccessible and remain hidden as deep memory, where they are secured from disturbing the conscious mind by a mental curtain. From birth on, the subconscious starts functioning and into it much of our thinking, including most event memories, will be transferred from the conscious mind.

With this description, we do not have to have two entirely different explanations for memory, one which fits those memories that form a constant part of our daily life, and the other which can explain memories relating to events and experiences in previous lives. It is the connection of mind with the new brain that sets up the barrier that will prevent previous life memories from entering consciousness. In the mind itself, this barrier does not exist. Full access to the mind, and therefore to all memories, will be available to mankind when full control of the mind in relation to the physical, emotional and mental bodies has been won. There are many who have started on that path already and, in the coming years, we shall see the recovery of deep memory being accepted as a faculty that can be developed by suitable mental training. Such training will be little different from that required now for playing long musical compositions, dancing complex roles, or delivering long speeches 'out of the mind'. We do not feel particularly astounded by these remarkable achievements; we know that the mind has many surprises in store for us. The recovery of memories of past lives is just one of them.

Memory will, therefore, become an increasingly important tool of the mind as we learn to increase its scope. Like the other tools with their potential development and increase in sensitivity, memory will add to the depth and penetration of our mental life. We shall then understand more fully the primacy of mental life over physical life, with all that this foreshadows for our social communications and contacts.

CHAPTER THIRTEEN
THE SENSES:
ACTION TOOLS

The five physical senses are the tools or instruments that give us all the information we can abstract from the physical world around us. Even the scientist depends on these for his research into the behaviour and constitution of matter, but he places between his senses and the object of his investigation, sophisticated instruments that are more sensitive than his unaided physical contacts. He scans the performance of these instruments with his eyes or ears, less commonly with one of the other senses. The senses report back to HQ, the mind, via the brain, whatever lies within their reach, and this flow of information about our environment allows us to build a coherent picture of the situation in which we find ourselves. We have learnt how to extend the limits of our senses in our everyday life by means of such things as field glasses or telescopes, megaphones, and many other similar gadgets, but so far we know that without the aid of complex instruments such as a television camera and screen, there are limits to the reach of our senses as we experience them at present, that we have to accept.

There is, however, a conviction growing among the thinking members of our race, that this is not quite the whole story, in fact, that it is only an infinitessimal part of the whole story. Science has revealed the non-solidity of what we take, from the reports of our senses, to be the fundamental concrete basis of our solid world. This confuses our interpretation of what we see, feel, and hear, so that we have to accept two incompatible explanations. There is also creeping in a belief that there is a range of sense perception that goes far beyond that of the physical senses.

We call this ability to transcend the contacts that our physical senses can make, psychic. It is rather rare, and those who don't possess it tend to be sceptical about the genuineness of what it is said to reveal. Those with psychic vision are able to 'see' at a distance, and the distance does not appear to have any limits, and to report scenes and actions with great clarity and detail. This is, of course, 'seeing' in the mind's eye, and for those with this kind of sense extension, there are mental equivalents of the other senses. We don't know how this sensitivity works, and scientists have not yet come to grips with the research necessary to find out.

These psychic senses, in addition to being able to make extended contacts on the apparently purely physical level, are able to penetrate to a level of matter existing at a higher vibration rate than can be discerned by our physical senses at all. Unfortunately, this kind of sensitivity is not usually fully under the control of the person exhibiting it, and he cannot be certain whether he will be able at any particular time and place to function as a psychic or not. Further, the information received by such sensitives is frequently unreliable, and this has led many to discount the ability and to charge those who profess to have it as fraudulent.

The trouble is that it is seldom possible to direct these extensions of the physical senses as they are now functioning, as we can the physical senses themselves. In fact, the position of this uncontrolled psychic ability is an apparent reversion of evolution. It is the common possession of the animals and primitive peoples, and is used as a natural back-up to the protection afforded by the physical senses, before the mind and intellect are developed. In primitive peoples it did not come under the conscious direction of the mind; the psychic sense being drawn out by the sense of danger or other pressing physical need. In our present state of development, we no longer need this automatic assistance, the developed mind has taken on the task of dealing with emergencies at its own level. The psychic back-up has therefore faded out.

What many of those with limited and usually uncontrolled psychic senses are demonstrating, is access to the sense stemming from the solar plexus that no longer functions normally in the human being, but is still the normal equipment of the animal. Those who realize that this sense is not under their control should desist from activity of this kind until such time as it can be directed and controlled by the mind. In its uncontrolled form, there is much danger to the individual who allows this energy to be directed through his body. I am thinking here more of the medium than the clairvoyant.

The faculties of spasmodic clairvoyance, clairaudience, and mediumship, are ones that we should have left behind on the evolutionary path. But there is always an overlap between the discarding of a faculty and the acquisition of a replacing one. It is possible, also, that those who still demonstrate this ability were powerful users of this kind of energy in previous lives. The reason why it appears not to be under control now, is that intellectual dominance is taking over from what has been dominance by the autonomic mind, but we have not yet progressed sufficiently to know and understand what it is that we are contacting, and how to set about its conscious control.

Must we then expect to lose the ability to extend the reach of the senses beyond the purely physical aspects of our world? By no means. The development of higher mind opens to our awareness realms of being and the perception of matter too fine to be contacted by our physical senses. This awareness will greatly increase the reports that the mind can make to the brain, as they will now include all that this new awareness can reveal. This will be received as a fuller description of the environment than was previously available, but a quite natural one; it will not seem that one is delving into the realms of the supernatural. The higher mind is able to contact distant scenes without the aid of the physical eyes, and to make all the other contacts that are made by today's sensitives, but under complete control.

Of course, there are some advanced human beings who already have this ability; and there are many who can make regular and certain contact with entities who are not in incarnation. There are fewer who have controlled and accurate psychic vision. These advanced individuals demonstrate the growing integration of the 'I', that is the 'knower' with the higher mind. They are signposts indicating that the individual is progressing towards becoming a soul-infused personality or, as the Buddhist would put it, becoming aware of the 'essence of mind'. This experience is recorded in the teachings of Hui Neng and Huang Po*. It is a state of being in which all the psychic faculties demonstrated by animals and primitive humans are greatly exceeded and available at will. It is a state towards which we are progressing as we fit ourselves to enter the Kingdom of God. What was available to an early race of mankind, will become a natural ability on a higher turn of the spiral of spiritual development. In the examination of all psychic phenomena, we must discriminate between those that are incidental, uncertain, and unreliable, and those that are the product of higher mind contact. The mind is not limited to what the physical body can ascertain. The contacts with reality made by the physical body are at present held within the restricted range of the physical senses.

In the human being, the senses are potentially capable of operating at three distinct levels, physical, psychic, and spiritual. They are the same senses, that is, they produce the same kind of results, but make their contact in different media. For instance, smell that can be sensed on the physical level gives us not only the scents we discern round us, but also the flavours of our food and drink. We tend to think that this is as much as we can possibly know of scent in our environment, but it is not so. The psychic sense of smell is capable, not only of detecting scents at a distance quite beyond the reach of the physical sense, but also reacts to scents that the physical sense cannot detect, because they are composed of matter finer than that for which the physical organ is designed. Similarly, the spiritual sense of smell will have as its field of contact a quite different character of

* *The Zen Teaching of Huang Po*, edited by John Blofeld (The Buddhist Society).
The Sutra of Hui Neng, edited by Christmas Humphries (The Buddhist Society).

information which is as yet beyond our interpretation. Just as the flavours of our food seem to be something different from the smells that are sensed in the nose, so the spiritual sense of smell will give us a sensation of something different yet again; it will be a new experience, and we shall not use it for our personal satisfaction, but for the purposes which the higher mind will have initiated.

Of course, the description given above applies to all the senses. While our awareness is limited by the reports of the physical senses we are, naturally, mainly involved in a physical response. The much wider field now opened up will influence our thinking and behaviour, and we shall begin to leave behind the purely physical satisfactions, and learn the truth of our status as a unity of consciousness within the mind of the God of our planet, and therefore the reality of brotherhood. Then the greater powers, which the controlled psychic senses and the burgeoning spiritual senses will bring to mankind, can safely be demonstrated. It is the emergence from the mire of materialism and its values that must come before the fuller beauty of the scene by which we are surrounded can be revealed.

Efforts to force the development of psychic powers which can be made through certain exercises and regimes are not recommended. Power before the spiritual maturity to handle it aright is a recipe for disaster. These powers must be allowed to develop through the lifting of the 'I' of the individual out of the world of material values into the world of spiritual insight. That is the only safe way.

For those who have not given thought to this concept of the expansion of the senses, it is difficult to understand that sight could apply to anything other than what the eyes reveal, or that hearing could be convincingly real when not received through the ears. But these extended senses are simply means of making contact with our surroundings. While the physical scenery of our life is all that the mind knows about, there is no incentive to look for other kinds of contact. But once the mind begins to reach beyond the purely physical, and entertains ideas which cannot be satisfied by the limited physical interpretation of our world, then the way is clear for the refined senses to come into being.

We know that the mind is capable of seeing and hearing

without having received information from the physical senses. In the case of seeing, we call this visualization or mind-picturing. But, of course, this ability applies to all the senses. We have powers to 'think-see', 'think-hear', 'think-feel', 'think-taste', and 'think-smell', that is, powers to create these impressions of our own volition and without the aid of the physical senses. There is nothing supernatural about the acquirement of the psychic senses; it simply means that a new kind of contact can be made with our physical surroundings, which utilizes finer matter than the physical senses are capable of detecting. These contacts leave impressions in the mind which are interpreted by the brain as equivalents of the products of the five physical senses. In fact, they are new perceptions and, as publishers often say, 'any resemblance to factual occurrences is entirely incidental'. We are receiving a quite different set of qualities of the scene or object, which the brain conveniently interprets for us in the form of easily recognizable symbols.

The same sort of addition to obtainable information occurs when the spiritual senses come into operation. A far greater extent of contacts becomes available to the mind. Those energies working behind the scenes, the hidden pressures that drive all creation along the evolutionary road, can be sensed and understood. The world becomes a much richer field for investigation and learning, and the understanding that this brings instils in the perceiver a deep longing to help mankind. This extension of awareness sets the seal of service on the life of the individual.

The senses, then, are the tools of the mind *par excellence*. Without them, the mind would have nothing to work on to develop its potentiality. We have now reached the stage where we must accept and understand the limitations of the physical senses, and become aware of the world of contacts that lies behind the coarse vibrations of our physical matter. We are like the audience of a television screen, trying to interpret a scene when only a small portion of one corner is visible. This is a puzzle game which has sometimes been shown, and is a close parallel with the way in which we regard our world as made up exclusively of those things which our physical senses can detect. We must now assume the attitude of the audience described above, who know how much more there is to be revealed, and can even imagine (visualize) the full picture from what is presented in the clue.

CHAPTER FOURTEEN
MEDITATION:
AN ACTION TOOL

It may surprise some that I am including meditation among the tools of the mind, but it is a very important one. Without meditation, the expanded awareness of the mind can only be achieved by the slow process of evolution. Taking up meditation is like introducing a new tool to a machine which will very greatly increase the speed of working and improve the production of the finished article. I do not want to discuss here the various forms of meditation or how it should be carried out. I would simply like to bring to the notice of my readers the significant value of learning the necessary technique of working with this tool of the mind, and the benefits that this will bring.

Meditation itself makes use of other tools, and these have first to be mastered before the technique can be developed. For instance, relaxation, breathing, concentration, repetition, and frequently mind-picturing are all subsidiary tools for this effort, first of all to control the mind, and then to open up new avenues of awareness.

It is known and accepted that, just like a muscle, we have to *use* the mind in order to increase its power and capacity. All our kindergarten and early school teaching should be aimed at this, and the dull repetitive methods, now scoffed at by some teachers, are very necessary for the orderly, logical side of the mind. This is the aspect of mind by which we conduct our lives until the higher abstract qualities begin to influence our thinking. For the mind does possess two distinct aspects, the rational and the abstract. It is rational thinking that directs our actions and the decisions of daily life, in the home, at work, and in recreation. It is the reliable packhorse which, by transferring so many of our learnt actions to the subconscious or autonomic mind, relieves us of much of the burden of getting around and doing things. The appearance of the abstract mind on the scene is a gradual process. Once it has established itself, the whole pattern of mind development changes. It must now be aimed, not at the extension of knowledge, but at the widening of awareness. This change is accelerated by the practice of meditation, which gradually opens a door of such significance that the whole of one's life is completely redirected. One is 'born again', an expression used not always with justification, but in this case truly expressive of the 'turn-around' that takes place. I cannot emphasize too strongly the tremendous step forward into new realms of being, of understanding, and of action, to which this relatively simple undertaking will lead.

The first requirement for meditation is a degree of mind control. About this there is, I know, a good deal of misunderstanding. Complete mind control is not possible, until the individual ceases completely to be drawn by the pull of the senses and the demands of the personality. That stage of development is still a long way off for most of us. What is required is a reduction of the interruptions by uninvited thoughts, and familiarity with the technique of deflecting them. It will be found that, however distracted the early attempts at meditation may be, the interruptions *will* become less and less. It is usually advisable for a meditator to begin with one of the special meditations aimed at learning the technique of checking interruptions. This may require only a few months or at most a year.

Having achieved the necessary degree of concentration, one can then embark on a new process that leads eventually to the extension of the mind's awareness. Proper understanding of the term 'awareness' is crucial to the success of this new kind of mind training, so that, in fairness to my readers, I must explain what I mean by it. I dislike definitions; they are so frequently convenient condensations, which always limit and constrict. They tend to put a fence round the meaning that a word or a phrase should have. Sometimes this is justifiable for 'shorthand' thinking, but if one accepts a definition as a guide to one's understanding, one should always know that the clearcut boundaries it expresses seldom exist in reality.

Awareness

Our awareness at present is very largely limited by the reports and messages we receive from our physical senses. These tell us of our physical surroundings, and the impact of our own and others' actions. We are aware of heat and sound, of being hit by someone's fist, and of the sense of comfort. There are awarenesses that are less compelling than these, such as ordinary hunger, tiredness, and physical well-being. Others still less demanding but which are common awarenesses, are such feelings as beauty, joy, satisfaction and many other mental reactions which are the result of physical contacts. The mind, in fact, creates its own fields of awareness as it begins to acquire information that fits into a coherent pattern. At present, nearly all these fields are the result of some mental reaction to a physical contact. They form the groundstuff of our daily life experience.

There are other awarenesses that are not dependent on physical sense contacts, but which are generated by mind alone. These are such things as justice, love (but not sexual attraction which so frequently limits the meaning of love), brotherhood, and Godness, that inner sense of divinity which is clouded by our polarization in the material world. For we do have a sense of divinity; the 'I' we are conscious of has its roots in the divine, and will, in time, develop a fullgrown awareness of the God within. The mind-born awarenesses I have referred to are products of the fringes of the higher mind. It is by meditation that we break through this fringe area to what at present lies hidden from our conscious thinking. This question of awareness is all important to our consideration of meditation, for it is meditation that opens up the mind to new awarenesses, which reveal completely new worlds of contacts from which to receive rich experience.

Some of us know, others suspect, that the many phenomena of what is called the 'paranormal' indicate that there is a great deal to be discovered that lies beyond the reach of our physical senses. It seems that there are other senses to which we give the name 'psychic', which allow us to see, hear, feel, taste, and smell, without prior contact by the physical senses. These are, in fact, an extension of our normal faculties but, as at present possessed by many, are not evidence of evolutionary progress. The animal world and primitive peoples possess psychic senses as a normal part of their equipment. We have gradually lost them as we have become more mentally polarized and less subject solely to our emotional nature.

At the present stage of the reaching-out by the minds of thinking men and women towards the understanding of the subjective world, these occasional human abilities to see and hear what is not physically based (at least, not by our understanding of what is physical), have a valuable role to play, for they demonstrate the existence of a world within our physical world, that must be taken account of in a description of our total environment. Science is looking at these phenomena with a critical eye, seeking for explanations that will fit into a somewhat expanded concept of reality as we now conceive it. They must be found, otherwise they and we shall be faced with a continuing and convincing demonstration of phenomena, that have to be classed as 'inexplicable' or 'not really existing'.

All of these psychic contacts have their counterpart in the world of spiritual energies. When the inner resident has been contacted by the mind, the largely uncontrolled phenomena of the psychic senses will be replaced by the fully controlled products of a higher form of contact which, for lack of a better term, we call spiritual. With this new ability for making contacts within the coarser substance of the physical world, we shall be employing the higher mind, and this will permit us to read and transmit thought at will. This higher aspect of the mind is fully latent within every human being, but we have not yet learnt how to construct the channel between it and the lower rational mind, and thence to the brain. Meditation is aimed at the process of constructing this channel.

The 'I' we feel to be ourself is defined and limited by our awareness. This awareness comes to us through the mind. For those who are still not clear about the position of the mind in our concept of the 'I', a few words may help. The mind, as we know it at present, is simply another sense, a sixth sense which acquires information from any source open to it. It is an instrument which acts as a sensitive plate, and transmits what is recorded on it to the brain. It is an instrument of knowledge. Up to the present time our knowledge has been limited largely by the information coming from the physical senses, but that is now changing.

The process of acquiring mind-control in meditation, is one of clearing this recorder of all those impressions being transmitted from the senses via the brain. When this has been achieved, it is able to record impulses more sensitive than those received from physical sources, because of their higher vibration, which can now be received from the higher self, the resident, or the soul. These can also be transmitted to the brain, and we have the situation where a new awareness is being born. This new sense of awareness changes the whole aspect of the 'I', because the knowledge of itself and its environment has been expanded to include a world of subtle influences previously unperceived. Naturally, while living in the physical world, the coarser impressions will still be perceived, but they will have lost the priority they previously enjoyed.

This, then, is the aim of meditation, the reaching out to a new field of knowledge coming direct from the resident, the soul, and bring transmitted by the mind to the brain. We have to accept, therefore, the existence of an entity, detached and apart from the mind, who seeks to use it as a means of transmitting knowledge to the brain. This entity is referred to in the Christian religion as the soul. It is this entity which stands behind the 'I' that we feel to be ourselves. The Buddhists call it the 'essence of pure mind'. It is only by meditation that we learn to make conscious contact with this entity, the real essence of ourselves.

Meditation, regarded as a tool, is a refining agent. It sharpens the mind by teaching it how to discard the relatively clumsy (but essential for existence in the physical world) activity of the rational concrete mind, and to make contact with the higher mind and its inexhaustible source of knowledge that comes from the intuition. It is the content of the mind itself that we are, by meditation, lifting to a new level of enlightenment. At this level, it can receive, carry, and direct a greater amount of energy, so that all the other tools I have written about, which are relevant to any particular mental activity, are of increased importance.

Meditation is gradually spreading throughout the western world, and this is a major step towards the further expansion of mind that is now due. But I doubt whether many of the new adherents to this technique know what it is that they are starting out to do. Unfortunately, we have, up to now, adopted almost without exception, one or other of the systems of meditation as practised in the east, where it has been practised for many thousands of years. These systems are not ideally suited to the mainstream of new meditators in the west with the exception of very few who may, through special circumstances, be able to adapt their psychological nature to the requirements of the eastern form.

The western temperament is greatly different to the eastern with its patient, easy-going acceptance of intense effort towards a very distant goal. The eastern meditator is taught that his search for enlightenment may require him to continue his efforts beyond this life, and perhaps many others too. The western meditator does not easily accept this kind of working towards an objective. He is eager to have a more easily attainable goal, a short-term aim, so that he can put into practice what he has gained through his meditation as he goes along. Not for him the resigned and patient attitude that his eastern brother is perfectly content to adopt.

There *are* meditation systems that limit the goal that the meditator is set. Each meditation form is designed for a certain period, maybe for a year or perhaps two. After that time, the limited goal aimed at should have become sufficiently a part of the understanding and aspiration to be put into practice in daily life. It is in the everyday thoughts and activities that spiritual progress is to be made. The physical environment is the field where the struggle takes place to put the new understanding to work in a man's relations with those intimate and close, as well as the rest of humanity. Each goal set by the meditation form takes the meditator a step further towards the main purpose of conscious contact with his true essence. The journey is taken in several stages, and at each stage he will have acquired a new outlook with which to adjust his thoughts and behaviour in the world of practical expression.

There are only a few systems of meditation that aim at this kind of progress, probably the best known of these is the Arcane School, started by Alice Bailey in the early twenties. The school only accepts students who are considered to be suitable, and their progress is carefully monitored. Their programmes, however, would not be suitable for the mass of new meditators. Something simpler, with targets set perhaps by Christian standards (i.e. not esoteric as in the Arcane School), is required for the general run of those starting out on the technique of meditation.

A committee of those who have experience of teaching meditation and who have no particular axe to grind, should have no difficulty in coming up with, say, six progressive programmes of meditation to be adopted as standard, and which would be suitable also for children from the age of ten to twelve. For when it comes to meditation, an adult who has had no experience has little, if any, advantage over a mentally active child of the ages I have suggested.

Something of this sort is badly needed, because of the proliferation of so many different methods of meditation. Some of them are excellent in their own way, others, however, have been 'invented' by teachers who set themselves up as gurus with the object of acquiring a large following of believers and, incidentally, often amassing a great deal of money in doing so. The number of different forms of meditation that are now being offered to the public is bewildering for the beginner. The start of meditation is very important; start right and it will be found that progress will come naturally.

I have had no experience of teaching meditation, but I give below a suggested list of the targets that might form the aims of the series of meditations of such a standardized method.

1. To acquire the necessary degree of mind control, anapanasati (concentration on the breathing). Something of this sort is essential before starting out on the targeted series.
2. The constitution of man: the three bodies.
3. The alignment of the three bodies, i.e. learning not to be dominated by the emotional body, as most of us are.
4. The understanding of light and love.

5. The alignment of the three bodies with the soul or essence.
6. The meaning of brotherhood and the service of humanity.

These are only my suggestions as to what might be set. They could form the basis on which the committee could discuss the matter. What must be done is to bring meditation to the masses of those now ready for it in a form that will fit in with their native temperament, and that can be taken up without having to surround themselves with an aura of eastern mystery.

The practice of meditation is of particular importance at this time, because it is the only way of bringing about the contact with the higher mind other than by the gradual process of evolution. The extension or expansion of the mind's awareness is far more important than the bare words 'contact with the higher mind' can convey, for it is nothing less than the establishment of the 'Kingdom of God' on earth, the time, that is, when men and women will be under the direction of the 'God within'. We have, up to now, tried to make our peace with the 'God without' — God transcendent — and not very successfully. To a much lesser extent have we aspired to make contact with the 'God within' — God immanent. That is now the proper role of religion and, to this end, meditation is the tool working directly on the *mind*, whereas, previously, the approach to God has been through the emotions. This is not to belittle the function of the emotions, which have played a valuable part in the development of the mystic. The future role of this part of the human being's constitution is of far greater import, and will gradually be developed over the coming years.

Meditation as a tool of the mind is, therefore, one which we must now bring into common use. In order to do this, we must make it easier for the beginner to find out how to start off. This means, incidentally, discouraging the 'guru hunting' that is so prevalent these days. The only guru we need to hunt is the one that lies deep within our nature, but now within the reach of our mind.

CHAPTER FIFTEEN
MENTAL MATTER:
AN ACTION TOOL

Mental matter is the most obvious and natural tool of the mind, though it is not generally accepted as such. In fact, it is not generally accepted as existing at all! Here, I know that I am treading on difficult ground, but the difficulty has to be faced. It would be more accurate to say that the mind is the instrument which works with mental matter, and this, in turn carries energy to its objective. Anyone who, from the start, is convinced that there isn't such a thing as this fine form of matter, should omit this chapter. Those with an open mind will, I know, read it because it is crucial to the connection of mind with thought, and how one thinks about the working of mind is very important to us all. I know that mind itself is not accepted by many; thought, for them, is held to be a secretion of the brain, rather as an endocrine gland secretes hormones, and this is felt to be a satisfactory explanation of thought, to replace that of a mind that cannot be proved to exist. I do not want to embark on this controversy so that, in what follows, I accept the fact of mind as quite separate from the brain, and working in a completely different medium.

With all the developments of science that we see around us, it should not be difficult to think of matter as being capable of existing in many different forms and at varying rates of vibration. Vibration is critical for our senses. We know this when considering the range of our sight and hearing. Raise or lower the vibrational rate from the rather narrow band which our senses can detect, and we can hear and see nothing. The same, of course, applies to matter, though we haven't yet been given a proof similar to that which exists for sight and hearing. But this proof will come. We do, however, accept matter of varying degrees of fineness, provided that it is capable of being detected, either by our senses alone, or aided by the instruments of science, but we are not consistent about this. We accept the existence of a gas, and would probably be prepared to agree that it consists of very fine particles of matter which we can't see, but can sometimes detect by smell or the effect it has on our physical bodies. It is not a very large step from this to the acceptance (perhaps only as a temporary hypothesis) of an even finer form of matter which is manipulated by mind, and is what we call thought. I would ask you to accept this suggestion provisionally for the purpose of reading what follows. You may find that it makes a great many things clearer, that before you were unable to understand. What we always have to do when increasing mental awareness, is to learn to regard the subjective as objective, and it is the first step in this process that proves difficult. This is the step I am now asking you to take, to regard thought as a form of matter finer than any other we know about, but still capable of carrying and directing energy.

This is the important concept that we are now considering, that thought is a transmitter of energy. That is the reason for my writing about tools of the mind, for they are the means of increasing the amount of energy that our thoughts can carry, that is, of making our thinking more efficient and more powerful.

We are not entirely without pointers in this direction. Many years ago, in the early twenties, I remember that Gamages, the well-known multiple store no longer in existence, sold, as an amusing gadget, a very light metal vane pivoted accurately on a needle point bearing and covered by a glass dome. It behaved in a strange way. If one put finger and thumb round the glass dome without touching it, and 'willed' the vane to go round clockwise, it would do so. One could then order it to stop and reverse the direction of rotation. I never saw any authoratative explanation of this phenomenon, but for all those 'ignorant' persons who played with it, it was assumed that the mind was exerting a force on the vanes which made them rotate. There may have been, of course, some other acceptable explanation, but it wasn't forthcoming.

More recently we have read accounts of a Russian woman who, under test conditions, was able to move a small inverted glass by simply concentrating on it. A few years ago I saw, at one of the May Lectures, a film showing the glass being moved and, although the film was not a very good one, it did seem to back up the account. Of course, the Russians may have been pulling a fast one over us, though I doubt it. If that was what it was, I think they would have taken the trouble to produce a much better film and present it rather more convincingly than they did.

There is another example much nearer home. We give mental instructions to our muscles every time we move any part of the body. These instructions are received by the brain and somehow, somewhere along the line, they are converted into minute electrical currents, which travel along the nerves that lead to the muscles that have to be activated. How does the original thought become transformed into an electrical potential (if indeed it does)? In his book *Blueprint for Immortality* (Spearman, 1972) Dr Burr relates the work he carried out over some thirty years recording the electrical potentials that exist around the human body, as well as other forms of life. These could not be measured until a specially sensitive voltmeter had been developed. The potentials exist at a small distance from the surface of the body, and could be detected without any physical contact with the electrodes. During his tests, it was found that thought could influence the reading of the voltmeter. Happy or sad thoughts, for instance, produced a deflection of the needle showing a change in the electrical potential. This was confirmed by tests on a number of people.

I have no doubt that there is a significant connection between thought and electricity. This is something which I hope some interested scientist will consider worthy of further research. Is thought itself, perhaps, a form of electricity? And if so, how does it make contact with the brain? In the examples given above, thought is clearly resulting in physical action. It may be that thought, impinging on a denser form of matter, becomes electricity. The amount of force that this thought/electricity combine can apply, depends on the nature of the thought. The more dynamic the thought, the more forceful the action. Our thinking sends out thought charged with energy, and this book is looking at the ways in which we can increase the energy our thought carries. All the tools about which I am writing require new techniques which enable us to put more power into our thoughts. Just as we can increase the energy carried by matter, for example, by giving it greater speed or greater weight, thus increasing its momentum, so can we and do we increase the energy carried by our thought. A few moments reflection would convince us that thought, whether directed outward in the form of words, or inwards in the form of ideas or intentions, can vary in the amount of energy it directs.

In a vague sort of way, we know how to increase this energy. We pay more attention to what we are thinking and we put more effort into our concentration. This is a direct parallel with giving matter more momentum. Concentrated thought is much more penetrative than vague and loose thinking. This we all know, but we probably haven't questioned why this is so. The answer is, of course, because it carries more energy, and it can't do this unless it is a form of matter. Science has already shown that very fine forms of physical matter, such as the atom and its many and various particles, carry great amounts of energy, and this has been demonstrated to the world in the explosion of the atomic bomb and in atomic power stations.

That there are other ways of releasing this energy without the disastrous results of an atomic explosion, we have been told by C.L. Kervran in his book *Biological Transmutations*. In this book, Kervran describes how micro-organisms are able to transmute one element into another, and that this process occurs in plants and in rock strata. The exchange of energy that is required in such processes is shown to be made possible by these micro-organisms, which are able to channel energy from the orbit of one element to that of another. Scientists, or some at least, accept the possibility of organisms much too small to be seem with the human eye, juggling with energy in this way, but hesitate to agree that thought, which manifestly carries energy, is a fine form of matter. The one concept is no more fanciful than the other. If we do accept this, it makes our effort to increase the amount of energy carried by our thought a rational, instead of an imaginative project. In our present stage of development, we are masters of rational thought but, as yet, have not taken this rational process as far as to explain the kind of medium we use for it!

How is increased energy applied to thought? First of all by removing all the obstacles I have described in earlier chapters, such as the interruptions caused by lack of adequate concentration. The way has to be cleared and, provided that this is done, the right preparations made, and the right tool for the job employed, then energy will flow in just as if you reduce the resistance of a wire carrying electric current, you will increase the current it can carry. Clear away all the obstructions to efficient thinking, use the right tools, and all the energy you need will be available at your direction, that is, when you will it to be so.

Readers may be wondering how mental matter compares with physical matter in its usefulness, seeing that we are surrounded by physical matter and our senses can contact it, and that these contacts give us all we know of our physical world. The answer is that it holds the important place of being *behind* the usefulness that we get from our physical senses, and that without it these contacts would be still-born. We are surrounded by it, but it exists at a higher rate of vibration than our senses can detect. Our thinking manipulates mental matter into thoughtforms which can be seen by a few people who possess psychic vision of this kind. Weak muddled thoughts, thinking that is not precise and thought through to some conclusion, all produce indefinite forms in mental matter. Such thinking has no chance of getting anywhere and, unfortunately, much of our thinking is of this kind. Positive, direct thought that is continued until it has gone as far as it can, the kind of thinking that covers the subject matter right through, leaving no part of it woolly or half defined, will produce clearly outlined thoughtforms composed of mental matter. When they are produced in this form, they are strong enough to become the basis of further action by the individual.

To the bare but well-defined thought, he then adds his desire to do something about it, generating enthusiasm and confidence that he has something worth working on. This kind of attitude naturally leads to physical action being taken. It may be action to create an organisation to carry through the project, or it might be the determination to embark upon the construction of some new device which his thoughtform represents. Whatever it may be, there is a clear line of action that must always be followed between the initial thought and the final physical appearance. The furtherance of some social activity, the creation of some work of art, or the more mundane production of some physical object, all have to be put through the same process. They all start with a positively formed thought, which must be sufficiently clear and well-defined to enable the rest of the process to take place.

It is from mental matter that cathedrals are built, books are written, and ideologies are designed and enforced. And yet we believe thought to be an airy-fairy non-substance, despite the fact that we also have to acknowledge that it is the most powerful force in the world! If we look at these two concepts dispassionately, we can see that they are impossible bedfellows. With the progress of rational thinking that has taken place during the last hundred years, and the pressure now mounting to take it fearlessly into the realms of the intangible, the nature of thought is one of the first things that will have to be brought within our rational frame. We have all the evidence from the process I have outlined above, and the pointers from our present knowledge of matter, to enable thinking men and women to put two and two together, at the very least as a hypothesis on which to build a potential scientific explanation.

The man in the street needs the official pronouncements of science, although he may not be able to understand them, to increase his accepted knowledge of the world in which he lives. Many others get this through their personal experience. The mental world is one which doesn't need expensive and intricate instruments for its investigation. We have within ourselves all that we need to unveil the higher reaches of mind, but we have, first, to reshape the personality in order to make it fit and able to respond to what the higher mind will reveal. That is not just a form of words with little meaning, it signifies the be-all and end-all of the extension of our awareness of our own nature and that of the world in which we live.

We cannot achieve these deeper contacts with reality until our personality nature has been changed, so that we can make use of them for the common good. The word 'personality' suggests that what is good for it is necessarily good for the individual, and we have become obsessed with the necessity of looking after its exaggerated desires. Of course, the personality, which is the only contact the essence of being has with the physical world, must be tended. It must be kept healthy, active, and efficient, but at the same time it must learn to be receptive to what is filtering down from the higher mind to the brain. The implications of this new knowledge will always be for the good of mankind as a whole, and the pressure behind the resulting action will be the sense of brotherhood, of one family, and of the wellbeing of all.

This is an attitude which can start in the home and in the place of work. It may seem a small change to make in one's thoughts and behaviour, but it is, in reality, a complete about-turn in the road that most of us are following. All this will come about through the realization that thought is real, it is matter; it has definite effects, and it cannot be kept private. When we are faced with the prospect of having to expose and share our evil and selfish thoughts, it will prove a great incentive to eliminate them!

CHAPTER SIXTEEN
CREATIVE IMAGINATION:
THE 'AS IF' PRINCIPLE;
AN ACTION TOOL

Probably the best known, if not the first, exposition of the principle of creative imagination, was the teaching of M. Coué which became known as 'Couéism'. The statement 'Every day in every way I'm getting better and better' was not just one of pious hope, it was one which, in the saying, generated and directed energy to whatever it was that was required to get better. It was, in fact, a very general indication that, if you want to *be* something, then think you are it already. If you want to become more considerate of other people and less concerned about your own wellbeing, you must be this in imagination. This means, of course, acting out your new character whenever the opportunity occurs. The more you can bring your imagination to bear on the events of your daily life, the more success will you have in bringing your character in line with what you want it to become. But you must sincerely want to make the change. It is no good saying to yourself 'I'm giving up smoking' when all the time you don't really want to do this. The counter-wish will take all the energy from the imaginative picture of yourself no longer smoking.

Any defect in character can be overcome by this method, and

it can be used in all sorts of minor problems. For instance, a man has to do a lot of public speaking and is always nervous before beginning, so that the first few minutes of his talk are halting and ineffective. He should imagine himself standing in front of his audience feeling dynamic and full of eagerness to begin, seeing himself as confident and completely at ease. After a few days of this exercise, he will find himself overcoming the hesitancy from which he had previously suffered. There is no situation to which this act of the creative imagination cannot be applied. It can become a habit so that one always imagines oneself doing things one is uncertain about with complete self-confidence.

How does this use of the creative imagination work? And is it limited to our reactions to tasks, duties and voluntary actions that we face every day? Before I answer these questions, I would like to digress a little to explain how important this principle is when it comes to the esoteric training of the individual for higher awareness, that is, for the expansions of consciousness that will bring into the scope of his mind those things of which we are only dimly aware at present; that, incidentally, will answer the second question. There are two ways of achieving this development. The first is by slow and gradual evolution, which has been, for the majority, the method up to the present. It has brought us, over millions of years, from the primitive state of animal man to our present one of developed emotional reaction, and increasingly efficient use of the mind with its quite startling intellectual power. It has now become possible for man to take into his own hands the further development that leads to greater knowledge, wisdom, and sensitivity, through influences that have not up to now been able to find a response in our materially orientated minds. This self-action towards greater maturity has to take the form of a new direction of mental exploration. It requires aspiration and patience. The technique that has to be used is the 'as if' principle ('as if' being a clearer and less profound-sounding description than 'creative imagination'). The principle is well known to all esotericists. It is employed in meditation, in one's daily actions (but not just for achieving character improvements), and it is a common tool of the mind that has to be brought into use whenever the mind has to delve into non-material realms.

It has a very definite result, this, to some people, rather

nebulous and wishful way of thinking. It does two things. First, it creates tracks along which energy can pass to effect the targeted change. And second, it changes the vibrational character of the thought being 'as iffed' to enable it to tune in to the higher aspect of mind that is being sought. These are not just fanciful extensions of something that already seems to be a bit of a fairy tale. They are practical results that occur in the energy world, that world of which we are still so woefully ignorant, but which our scientists are beginning to investigate seriously. The creative imagination *does* open up a channel for thought energy to travel along, just as the creative imagination of the designer of an underground system starts the ball rolling for the construction of a tube along which trains will travel. Nothing can be achieved in the physical world unless it is first visualized in the mind in the varying degrees that creative imagination works. In the application of the 'as if' principle to mind expansion, however, we are dealing with mental matter that does not necessarily result in physical correlations, at least, not in results that we can observe like the construction of a tube railway, but the transference of conscious thinking to a higher level will inevitably affect the physical vehicle over which the mind holds sway.

So that my answer to the first question 'how does it do it?' is that it works, as the mind always does when using the creative imagination, through the pictured image gradually being impressed on the conscious mind until it 'possesses it'. But until we have the conscious knowledge and experience of creating in mental matter, we have to have the confidence that channels *are* being laid down and energy *is* being directed by the act of our thinking. We have to have the same sort of confidence when creating anything in the physical world, but, because we have previous experience of this, and can see the result of such creation all around us, it does not seem strange that actual physical forms are the product of the creative thought of a single man. We have to take a 'giant step' from the physical to the mental. We have to accept the reality of energy-charged thought, and we have to accept that thought can be creative on *its own plane* and will develop perceptions that stem from the higher mind.

The esotericist knows this from the experience of those who

have 'gone before'. He knows that he is embarking on what is, to him, a new course, but it is one which is well channelled. The small signs of progress are marked, and the changes within himself that he will encounter are forecast. Nevertheless he has only himself to rely on. Information can only be transformed into knowledge when experience has confirmed it, and into wisdom when it has been put into practice in his daily living. This is the rule under which the esotericist works. The mind is not to be burdened with dogma; it has to be its own master. This is the way, too, in which Buddhist teachers pass on their knowledge. 'Don't accept it from me; carry out your meditation as you have been instructed and you will learn for yourself. Knowledge handed down is only of value when it has been confirmed by inner perception'. Thus spoke my Buddhist meditation master in Burma. It was wise counsel. It is essential, when embarking on the path of seeking higher awareness, where the information received has no proof, no demonstration except what comes from one's inner experience, to have confidence that this inner confirmation will be forthcoming, and to wait patiently for it.

The 'as if' method of making progress is a temporary, fragile bridge constructed, at first, with a certain amount of hesitation; but once one has experienced the result, confidence is quickly gained, and one can begin to use the method as the vital tool of the mind that it is.

The creative imagination works through mind-picturing. It is the mind-picture that forms the channel for the energy it generates. What is being created may first be projected as an idea to be transformed into a plan. At that stage, the rational mind has to take over and, still working with mind-pictures, it is this part of the mind that will convert the plan into objective reality. So does all creation take place. Increase your ability to construct mind-pictures and your familiarity with the 'as if' procedure, and you will increase your creative output in whatever field you work.

Both of these abilities are valuable tools which the mind has to take up, practise, and work with, before their full potential can be realized. One doesn't expect to pick up a golf club and produce a perfect shot at first try. We are too ready to treat the mind as something already completely developed and incapable of being stretched. We unconsciously set limits to the kind of

knowledge we can acquire; some do this consciously through
religious conviction or scientific statements of facts as they
believe them to be. One can, of course, pull in new information
about this and that, provided that it doesn't attempt to bypass
the conventionally set limits, but the idea that new facets of the
mind can be opened up to give us new perceptions is not so
readily accepted.

The future development of the mind lies in just this kind of
expansion. For this, we have to learn to use the imagination as a
tool. In the past, we have used it exclusively to reminisce over
what might have been, or to cast a wishful-thinking glance into
the future. This doesn't do anything except feed the emotional
pressures of the present. It is a static and harmful way of using a
feature of the mind that is essentially dynamic, constructive,
and creative. Instead of letting imagination rule us, we have to
bring it to heel and then direct it to wherever we wish to create.
This 'as if' technique may sound tentative, feeble, unconvincing,
and merely another version of wishful-thinking. It is nothing of
the kind. It is bursting with latent power, and when it forms part
of the daily use of one's mind, it instils a joyous confidence that
before was lacking. These two words 'creative imagination' are
by far the most important in this book. If a reader decides to test
out what I have said for himself, he will, by that alone, have
made the reading of the book worthwhile. I have only placed it
after concentration and mind picturing in this discussion of the
mind's tools, because without these two it cannot function.
They form the chuck or the screws that hold this powerful tool
in place.

Learn to use the creative imagination now in all the little
things of the day's routine, and you will find that when you
want to use it to open up the expansion of mind that all are
waiting for (but most of us unconsciously), you will have
tempered a tool for your mind's use that will surprise you in the
extent of its creative drive.

CHAPTER SEVENTEEN
TENSION:
A SETTING-UP TOOL

The word 'tension', frequently met in the phrase 'a point of tension', is commonly found in esoteric literature. I think that many people either do not understand what it means, or perhaps believe that it is something they will recognize when they have progressed further with their esoteric studies. In reality, points of tension are common in our daily lives, but they are not given this somewhat grandiose description!

We experience three kinds of tension; physical, emotional, and mental. Of course, all tension is in the mind; it is the agent that produces it that varies. Probably the most obvious example of physical tension is the use of torture to extract information from unwilling individuals. It also exists, to a lesser extent, in the mind of the athlete tense on the starting-blocks waiting for the gun. I need say no more about this kind of tension as it is the common run of our experience.

Emotional tension is also the lot of our daily life. Strangely enough, the tension produced by emotion, unlike the emotion itself, is more often destructive than constructive, and it is frequently regarded as the prelude to some unpleasant physical reaction. It is because it is continually associated with the personality, that it is not generally a constructive pressure for spiritual maturity. It is, in fact, usually a conflict with something that is threatening the prestige or the security of the personality.

From our daily experience of emotional tension, we learn to trace its source and we note its gradual build-up to a point where our equanimity is seriously disturbed. Before that stage is reached, the more mature individual is usually able to check the further build-up which would inevitably lead to an emotional explosion. However, if the build-up to a peak is not prevented, the growing tension will result in a flare of temper often accompanied by violence. This is the natural result of uncontrolled emotional tension. It is the same for all potential tension of this nature, whether it be generated over a short period, or a long one of nagging worry or irritation. Initiation, build-up, and release, that is the programme for all tension, however originated. Not all tension, of course, leads to explosive results, some is dissipated through the originating cause being removed.

It is this kind of build-up, culminating in a peak where something has to happen, to which the esoteric 'point of tension' refers. Once the subject matter of the tension can be dissociated from the personality, it is either dissipated straight away, or is controlled and not allowed to build up. That applies to both emotional and mental tension. In this conscious build-up and handling of the peak point, tension becomes a most potent tool of the mind.

We are continually experiencing these moments of tension during our daily life, but the really constructive use of mental tension is mostly overshadowed by the more powerful emotional tensions which, because of the domination of our emotional nature, receive prior claim to our attention. Mental tension has to be worked on by the rational mind. It has to be consciously developed; it has to be used as a tool and fed to the subject, as a cutting tool is gradually fed to the metal being formed. This is neither possible nor desirable in the case of physical or emotional tension.

There is, however, a close parallel between the mental world and the physical. The engine of a car works through the balancing of tensions. The force of the explosion of the petrol vapour in the cylinder-head produces a tension which is relieved by the movement of the piston. The switching on of a light produces an electrical tension in the filament of the bulb, which is relieved by the heating and lighting up of the filament. Mental tension is developed by reaching out for some knowledge, some solution to a problem, or some new awareness. Gradually pressure is built up to draw aside the veil that is shrouding the new perception, until a fine balance is achieved between the urge to acquire the sought after goal, and the remaining obstructions in the way of achieving it. This is the tension that must always precede the acquisition of new knowledge or new awareness.

We speak of tension as the producer of physical ills, but this is, of course, unrelieved tension. There is a point in every kind of tension when it must be released. If one is pursuing new knowledge or new awareness, each peak of tension will extract from it what one is ready to accept. It is no good holding the tension beyond this point in the hope that there will be a continual flow of revelation. One must develop the sense to know when enough has been received for the next step. Holding the tension when nothing more can be received, because the searcher is not ready for it, will result in a serious imbalance. We know how this kind of imbalance, caused by continual anxiety or fear, can have serious results on the functioning of the body. When unrelieved tension exists in the higher reaches of the mind, it is the mind itself that will suffer from the imbalance it causes.

At present, we are mostly manipulated by tension. We have to learn to manipulate it to our advantage. This is important at the present stage of our development, because many are becoming conscious of the tension caused by spiritual aspiration, that is, the conscious intention to make contact with higher mind. With experience will come the recognition of the point where a response must be called forth from the higher mind. At this point, a relaxed receptive attitude is essential to open the path for the awaited revelation. It is a process of pressing, and keeping the pressure on until it has reached a critical point, and then relaxing and being ready to receive. It is a process of which many will be aware, though they may not describe it in quite these terms. It is demand and response, invocation and evocation, a natural law of which we have, up to now, not taken much notice.

Tension is something of which we are very much aware. It usually has an adverse connotation, and is looked on as the cause of both physical and psychological ills. It is something to be avoided. We take pills to do this, or we learn relaxation routines. At all costs, we mustn't be tense. That is, of course, a very one-sided view of the function of tension, without which we could not make decisions or progress in any field of our life's activities. We have been led to it by our familiarity with emotional tension and the unpleasantness it can cause. Both emotional and mental tension produce drive, but that of the emotions is usually destructive, while mental tension is frequently a prelude to invention and creative production of some sort. If we take note, we can observe the generation of tension when we embark on some mental activity for the solution of a problem, the creation of a work of art, an organisation, or the achievement of a goal that requires careful planning and persistence. In most of these activities, a point of tension is reached when the result should be forthcoming. The pressure for the solution has drawn out the answer from the deeper recesses of the mind, or the searching activities have reached a climax. This is a point of great importance. The maximum effort has been expended, and further effort would be unproductive.

We have to learn, first of all, to recognize these points of tension that occur in our mental lives, whether they be of the mundane kind or spiritually engendered. One has to be aware of the process going on. With mentally caused tension, which is what we are concerned with, this is not always easy. But, as we increasingly make contact with the higher mind, it will become more readily recognized.

The knack of consciously relieving the pressure and the confident expectation of the answer in clear understanding of what is being sought, are attitudes of mind that practice will make effective. But the revelation will not be instantaneous. In the waiting, one must be patient. Those who regularly review a difficult problem before going to sleep at night and find the answer presented to them in the morning, do not necessarily wake up with an 'eureka!'; they may have to wait until later in the day when, out of the blue, the solution flashes into their mind. This is, in fact, a good example of creating a mental tension, releasing it by going to sleep, and waiting confidently for the result.

In the case of emotional tension, it is a useful exercise to learn to be a 'watcher', observing the antics of the personality, and not associating one's true self with them. If one is successful in this, the peaks will never lead to the explosive release, instead they will be damped down by the knowledge that they do not stem from the true self. As we become familiar with the process of the build-up of emotional tension from the outsider's point of view we can, with real benefit, turn our attention to the corresponding process that takes place in the thinking of the concrete and higher minds. At present, when we are unaware that tension exists and is being built up, we allow the pressure to develop until something 'blows'. At the other extreme, we do not develop the quality of aspiration that is necessary for the tension to arise. The urge towards the goal is not sufficiently pressing, so that no tension is generated and no progress is made.

Once we become conscious of this process, it should develop into a successful technique by which all our mental undertakings are carried out. It is, in fact, the natural law of mental development. Aspiration, urge, tension, and release. Then the sequence is repeated on a higher turn of the spiral, with each new cycle ending in a further step forward in the search for truth. Each point of tension is a minor crisis, but like all crises, they are not dangerous if the method of dealing with them is understood and followed.

CHAPTER EIGHTEEN
THE INTELLECT:
AN ACTION TOOL

We live in an age which is demonstrating great intellectual development. Most of us believe that the intellect expresses the peak of the mind's potential, but it is really only a half-way house. It is where the training of the mind takes place to enable it to interpret and make use of knowledge coming from higher sources.

Although immensely powerful, the intellect is very limited in its sphere of action. It does not and cannot serve up new knowledge. It receives information from many sources, all via the reports of the senses, mainly in seeing and hearing things. By means of various devices such as memory, inference, and deduction, it moulds these reports into usable knowledge. In fact, it is simply a tool manipulating items of information into useful forms. It has developed over millions of years to become the formidable apparatus of thinking that we so readily recognize in the eminent men and women in various fields of activity.

We are going through this long nursery stage of perfecting the working of the intellect for two reasons. The first is that it eventually has to become automatic, and before that can happen, as has already happened with that part of the subconscious mind that we call the autonomic mind, it must become *familiar* (as must a passage to be played by heart on the piano), so that the subconscious mind can accept it and operate it. The second is that we shall have to rely on the intellect to interpret the knowledge that is now occasionally available to us from the intuitional mind, and which will increasingly be so in the coming decades. For the intuitional mind doesn't work, as does the concrete mind (which is that part of the mind using the tool of the intellect), in words and phrases, it works with ideas, ideas that are unexpressed, germseeds of thought, a new kind of thinking of which we, as yet have no experience. It is because the intellect will have this task of interpreting knowledge received from the higher mind, that its full potential must be developed.

The intellect is not the end of the reach of our minds, far from it. However highly developed, it is still a thinking– mixer training to become automatic. It sorts, combines, and extracts, in much the same way as does a computer. It does not create; recreates, perhaps, reforms and reconstructs. The artist uses his intellect to find the right words with which to express his meaning, or the right mix of paint, or to manipulate with his intellect whatever medium he is working in, to express the idea that has come from his link with the intuition. The genius works in the same way; he must use his intellect to precipitate, so to speak, the fruit of his genius.

Why do we need this long time for the continued development of the intellect? That is a question which leads to an explanation of how the evolution of the human being is being carried out. It is the intellect that uses the tool of discrimination. It sifts and recommends, according to the criteria that it is given to work with. And it is the criteria we use in the various acts of discrimination that determines our position on the path towards spiritual and mental maturity. The intellect has the function of abstracting and serving up. It is not itself the chooser. It is given the two sides of a question to decide on and the bias that quite frequently goes with them. It then recommends, either on logical grounds or, if the bias is strong enough, it will find grounds to support it. It is powerless itself to stop any particular decision being made on any ground; the resident, the thinker, always has the last word.

We have to look therefore to the resident himself for the reason behind the long development period required for a fully mature intellect. If we cast our minds back to the behaviour patterns of four or five hundred years ago, that were accepted as normal and approved of by the masses, whether it concerned behaviour towards one's fellow men or the animal world, one can understand how valuable a well developed intellect must have been to the ruthless power-seeker, and how evil men of great intellect triumphed. Even today, one does not have to look far to see the same kind of misuse of intellect in every walk of life. The intellect is not to blame. A machine tool can be used as readily for cutting up a treasured article as forming a valuable piece of furniture.

The intellect is a very dangerous tool in the hands of the spiritually undeveloped person, and that is the trouble. We are all of us, or very nearly all, spiritually undeveloped. All our discrimination is loaded by judgements based on personality. We have not yet found the basis for making unbiased judgements. We can only refer back to the 'I', and that is still, at best, only a faint reflection of the spiritual centre we *can* all contact, and at worst, a jumble of physically generated selfish reactions.

Until we have become spiritual beings, we cannot be trusted with the power that is generated by the intuitional mind. This progress and the progress of the intellect towards its full potential must go in parallel. When the base from which we operate has been lifted from the physically orientated 'I' to the real essence of our being, then the intellect will be found to have reached the limit of its development. In plain words, we must be able to make conscious contact with the essence of our being, the soul, that which at present stands behind the 'I' as we now know it; we must encourage soul to dominate the 'I'. Until this happens, we shall have no sure yardstick on which discrimination can rely.

Once we have made this contact and can remake it at will, and that only happens gradually, our choices will begin to reflect a consciousness of the real brotherhood of man and of all creation. It will express the sense of unity of a spiritual being instead of the separativeness of a physical one. It really is as simple as that. A spiritual being is one who has made contact with his essence, and whose thoughts and actions are directed by a new 'I' in which the personality has little say. We have to struggle to become a spiritual being; it is not done by waiting for the light to shine. It has to be a determined, relentless pursuit of the real, and a letting go of the unreal.

But how is one to tell the difference? How does one know what to let go? That is the intellectual interpretation of the result of conscious contact with the essence of one's being. This is what the intellect is being trained for, to work in conjunction with the pure mind essence of the individual; some would wish to call this the soul, but pure mind essence gives us as good an idea of how we should think of it as any other description. It is doubtful whether many people have any idea of how to think of soul. It is a word that is used by most of us as a convenience. It stands for all that we do not understand about our real self, the self that we are told constitutes our essence, but of which we have no awareness. For the intellect to interpret the knowledge that comes from the intuitional level of mind correctly, it must be free from mistakes and clumsy working. It must be able to do its job as the autonomic mind does, where failures can mainly be attributed to inheritance of one kind or another, and wrong behaviour. With the new knowledge that will flow down from the higher mind, wrong interpretation by the intellect could produce much graver results than anything that occurs to the physical body through conflict between the conscious and autonomic mind. The training of the intellect is still, therefore, of vital importance to our future development, and with it must go the gradual supplanting of the personality dominated 'I', by the conscious awareness of the pure essence of mind, of the soul. Until this happens, it would be too dangerous for us to be in tune with the power-giving knowledge that the intuition has in store for us.

This requires a programme of self-development for which there must be an inner urge. It is not wisely undertaken, as some courses of mental development promise, in order to give one greater influence over one's fellow men, or greater riches, or even a more satisfying life. All such improvements only serve to accentuate the position of the personality, and increase the power of its dominance. A turning away from the personality is required; this starts as a turning inwards until consciousness meets the explosively expanded awareness of total unity, not just the intellectual understanding of unity, and draws within its orbit the whole of creation at all its varying conscious levels. The reaction to this experience is the urge to contribute to the lifting of one's brothers in mind from the pain and suffering that the lack of this vision entails. Not for greater personality achievement is the new knowledge and power sought, but to aid one's brothers to find and tread the difficult road that lies ahead, a road that leads to greater and greater fulfilment. But how to do this? How shall this vital contact be sought and made?

This book is not the place to detail the action that must be taken in order to prepare oneself for this tremendous step forward. It requires dedicated study and regular meditation. There are many sources from which the right information on both these requirements can be obtained. Because meditation is rapidly becoming a rather common activity, it is necessary to say that the meditation undertaken must be the right form. It must have progressively achievable objectives. The meditator must know exactly what he is aiming at. The commonly taught eastern forms are not suitable. This has to be said, because right meditation is the key to right progress. Once started on the path of learning and meditation, the student should find his aspiration generating a momentum that will carry him through obstacles to his progress, and the difficulty of comprehension encountered on the way. It is a constant challenge, a challenge to one's mind and to the organization of one's daily life, but we thrive on challenges; they are the spur to greater effort, and bring out the potential that we hardly know exists. All along the way, it will be found to be rewarding work, to open up avenues of interest and new fields of worthwhile activity. I am here definitely indicating that there is a way to release the full potential that we all have as spiritual beings; that a life of working in the light instead of groping around in the mist of ignorance is available to all of us. It is an exciting enterprise, and anybody who sincerely desires to embark on this adventure will have no difficulty in being set on the path. It then only needs patience, perseverance, and persistence.

CHAPTER NINETEEN
INTUITION:
AN ACTION TOOL

Intuition has come to be regarded as an explanation for the seemingly irrational whims of women and, to a lesser extent, the hunches and sudden ideas that come to us without apparent previous thinking. That intuition, as we at present experience it, is the occasional direct contact with a higher level of mind than that which we employ in our normal daily rational thinking, is probably a new suggestion for some. But so it is.

Of the three ways in which the mind can transmit information to the brain, instinct, intellect, and intuition, only the intellect is under our conscious control. The functions which instinct controls were once consciously initiated, but have long since sunk below the threshold of consciousness. Intuition is the word we use to explain those ideas that come to us 'out of the blue'; it is information that we are unable to call on at will. It is not at all a precise method of obtaining information; in fact it is so unpredictable and so rarely experienced, that we can seldom be confident that it *was* the intuition from which the idea sprang, and not just the result of a previous train of thought. Nevertheless, it is a most important aspect of mind's potential. We must assume that what it is possible to experience now, although uncontrolled, will, in due course, become a major, completely controlled function of the mind.

What is the source of intuitional knowledge, and how do we make contact with it? I have written earlier of 'higher mind' as that aspect of mind which creates abstract thought, as opposed to the 'lower mind', which we make use of to handle the rational and logical processes we need in daily life. Although the distinction between these two aspects of mind may not be clear at first thought, it will be realized that the action of a child putting different shaped blocks into their respective holes in a frame, requires a completely different function of mind than say, a discussion on the validity of 'Ockham's razor' (see note on page 63).

There comes a time when the kind of sequence of thought that relies on information from the senses, or follows lines that have been set out by reason, is no longer adequate, and a different kind of thinking has to intervene. This changed form of thinking is what is called the 'higher mind' and, although we may only have touched it's lower strata, it will, if developed, take us right up to mental heights, where we can contact intuitional knowledge at first hand and at will. In its higher reaches, the mind has access to a vastly increased store of knowledge without recourse to any of the senses. Our fleeting experiences of intuitional awareness give us an indication of this access to direct knowledge that lies within the sweep of our minds.

There is no need, in this functioning of mind, to rely on the senses or the logical, inferential, deductive, and other processes of the mind, in order to acquire the knowledge we may be seeking; it is already there, within the reach of the mind, waiting only to be selected.

We shall gradually become intuitionally aware as we begin to live more in the higher mind, and many of the actions which the lower mind has to take care of will become automatic. We can see how this will happen in the performance of the computer, which can undertake many of the logical processes of the mind in the sorting and selection of information. It will become possible for us to tune in to a field of awareness where all knowledge is stored and select what is required for our questing thought, just as we now can select from memory a person's name, the combination of a lock, or the way to the railway station.

Over many years, this process of using the intuitional mind will become more and more the common run of mental activity, and the more utilitarian intellectual processes will sink below the threshold of consciousness, as instinct has done. This is exactly what happened to all the processes now handled by the autonomic mind — that part of the subconscious mind that looks after the functioning and maintenance of the involuntary systems of the body. One by one, these became so ordered that conscious control was no longer necessary, and each organ carried out its function by means of a kind of mental tape. These tapes are the result of continual conscious instructions given over many millions of years, which have become, through repetition, engrained on the mind of the part of the body concerned. Just as the conscious instructions to the fingers in playing a musical phrase can become automatic through repetition, so have the working requirements of these bodily parts become independent of conscious mental activity.

One can imagine a time coming when *all* the intellectual processes that we now undertake consciously will sink below the level of consciousness, and our active conscious life will be transposed to the intuitional level. We can assist the entry of intuitional awareness into the field of consciousness by using the creative imagination within the higher mind to form an impression of the intuitional level, and to guide its products down into the brain. This sounds difficult, as do all activities of the creative imagination, until they are tried. The creative imagination is immensely powerful; all it needs is encouragement, and perseverence. It is a long road to the goal of that stage of development — a very long road by the normal process of evolution — but it can be shortened by conscious effort. We have arrived at a point in our development where evolution need no longer be blind. We have developed the mental power to assist it in the right direction, and thus to avoid the setbacks that wrong paths blindly followed have caused in the past. Intuitional awareness is our next mental goal.

We have, then, to be constantly aware of the possibility of receiving intuitional information, and to maintain a mental attitude of expectation and encouragement. In this way we shall be more likely to recognize it when it comes. It will become a tool of overriding importance once we are able to call on it at will. The knowledge it will reveal will be certain, not in any way subject to doubt. Its very nature will ring of truth. We shall be able to distinguish clearly between the two types of thinking; they will be as different as chalk from cheese. This will be partly because the thought that comes in this way will not be associated with previous thinking, and this virgin character will be sensed by the new discriminatory power that the mind will have acquired. It will also be because the 'I' will have made conscious contact with the higher mind, and will therefore be able to trace the descent of intuitional thought along this contact to the lower mind and thence to the brain.

This new quality of thought will come only as a gradual process. Intuitional flashes will become more frequent until a familiarity with this kind of thinking is established that will enable it to be called on at will. As this is happening — probably over a period of thousands of years — certain aspects of intellectual thinking will be becoming automatic. We are, of course, progressing in this way all the time, but we do not notice it. We don't have to add three and three by an intellectual effort, memory does it for us. Any learned intellectual process becomes an automatic response to a mental instruction or to recognized stimuli.

All one's early physical movements as a child required conscious intellectual sequences, but these rapidly became subconscious. The intellect is being trained all the time to go automatic. As this process quickens, it will leave the conscious mind freer to receive thought from that source of knowledge that we now call the intuition, but which will then be recognized as a part of the higher mind. The mind has to be freed from the tasks that the daily round brings, just as it had to be when the control of the bodily functions were its prime concern, and these were gradually being transferred to a part of the mind below the conscious level. At present, the constructive activity of mind is intellectual, and we tend to think that this is the ultimate achievement of mind. The peak of intellectual ability is still far off, but this, too, is only a milestone to be passed on our way to becoming a functioning intuitional being.

CHAPTER TWENTY
PURITY:
A SETTING-UP TOOL

In the last but one of the tools of the mind that I wish to discuss, we are approaching the perfecting of mind which will enable its full power to be used at will. In order to reach this stage, a very drastic readjustment is necessary, and this will not happen until the individual has learnt to be harmless in the truest sense of the word. The matter is stated quite clearly in Mabel Collins' *Light on the Path* (Theosophical Publishing House, 1972). In the second paragraph of the book are the words 'Before the voice can speak in the presence of the Masters it must have lost the power to wound.' Behind the voice is, of course, the mind. It is the mind that must become powerless to harm. We are talking, therefore, of a highly spiritual being in whom the demands, the sensitivities, and the importance of the personality have lost their significance.

Before I discuss the purification of mind, some reference should be made to the physical spring cleaning that must precede this. For work on the mind to be successful, it must be given a body in which to manifest that is free from the poisons and pollutions of excessive and careless living, as far as this is possible. This should not take the form of a categorical disbarring from all physical pleasures, but rather a temperate attitude to all those habits which can so easily become harmful if overindulged in. This must be left to the common sense of the individual. There is no necessity, for instance, to abstain from all alcohol, to become a vegetarian, and to refrain from dancing and singing, as the Buddhist monk has to. These are choices which the individual must make for himself. What is needed is a practical form of living that avoids those excesses that harm the efficiency of the body, and thus affect the vital coordination between mind and brain. All mental concepts have to be brought down to the brain if they are to be given practical effect. It is no good developing an enlightened mind if it has to work through a diseased or impaired brain. In maintaining a healthy body through clean living, we can ensure a brain capable of responding to the aspirations of higher mind.

Why is it that the purification of the mind is necessary before its full power can be exploited? Why is it that, in our imperfect state, we cannot draw on this source of power to be used for good or ill as we will? These are pertinent questions because the power *is* there.

The practical answer to these questions is that it is all a matter of channels. A boiler with a head of steam and blocked tubes to carry the steam pressure to the engine it is to drive, is powerless until the tubes are descaled. We are in a similar condition and have to clear the channel for the transmission of mental energy from the mind to the brain. In the rather inefficient way in which we use the lower rational mind, we can see this happening. There is so much interference with thought, so many stimuli fed in via the senses, so much idle and uncontrolled chattering, that we find the greatest difficulty in holding the mental channel clear so that a desired thought can be given all our attention. If this is so with the lower mind, how much more obstructive of the finer thought originating in the higher mind must all the activities of the lower mind be, both deliberate and unconscious.

The channel-clogging that results from the uncontrolled activities of the lower mind can be cleared by a systematic effort to acquire mind control. A degree of mind control must be achieved before meditation practice can become fruitful, and meditation is essential to the completion of the process of clearing the way between the lower and higher minds. There are various exercises aimed at developing the kind of control that is necessary for serious meditation, all of which may appear somewhat tedious, unless one is convinced of the necessity for eliminating the inefficiencies of this wonderful instrument the mind. As one perseveres and becomes aware of the tricks the mind plays in order to avoid control, the exercise develops into a determination to decide who is master. This is a real challenge, and most people feel that it has to be met.

The development of mind control is the first requirement for increasing the power of the mind; it clears away most of the obstructions that interfere with the efficient working of the lower mind, but until something else is added, it cannot do more than this. The rational mind can only rationalize on the information and understanding of the situation that is given to it to deal with. A period of learning is necessary to confirm the existence of the higher mind and to acquire information as to what it holds.

The next step is to provide the mind with more factual information about the constitution of the human being, and his relation to the rest of creation. This is a slow business, but it is essential to learn of man's potential and of his true relationship to the rest of humanity, the animal, vegetable, and mineral worlds, in order to provide the background and impulse for the effort of clearing the channels to the higher mind. It is only when we realize the unity that lies behind all the diversity with which we are presented by the physical world, that we are able to readjust our values. This readjustment affects primarily the significance that we attach to the personality which, up to now, has been the centre from which these values have been assessed. There must be this dramatic change round. There are many, of course, who have done this without going through the long process of learning — Mother Theresa, for one, who exudes a simple natural love for her fellow beings in distress. This expression of the sense of one's 'belonging' brings with it a new quality of love, love for all creation centred on the true essence within the outer physical shape.

The information on which to form a new idea of the human being's position within the totality of creation, and the intelligent direction of evolution, has been given out during the past century. Lately this has been added to with a wealth of detail by the Tibetan, Djwhal Khul, in the books written down by Alice Bailey and published by the Lucis Press. Anyone with an active perceptive mind can learn from these books about the hierarchy of very advanced spiritual intelligences, which watches over and influences mankind to make the choices that will lead to the expansion of consciousness. With this expansion will come a growing awareness of the themes that will encourage the synthesis towards which we are progressing — love and intelligence. These mighty energies are those which are needed to overcome the predominant sense of separateness that divides humanity, resulting in selfishness, a desire for the wrong things, and a materialism that grips us and gives us the short view of life's purpose.

Learning of the true facts of our being and our existence within a living world, widens the channel of communication leading to the higher mind. It is this channel which, when fully developed and cleared of obstructions, will give us free access to the intuition with its store of knowledge and understanding. The act of clearing this channel is brought about by a new vision, new purpose, and a new way of life, and nothing less than this will succeed. This is where purification becomes the tool of quality that opens up fields of activity for the mind that cannot now even be imagined. The whole life of the human being is then changed, from one being mainly personality centred to one directed outwards to humanity and the life within the lesser creations. When one's attention is redirected in this way, the actions that result are characterized by unselfishness in the broadest interpretation of the word. The previous significance of the lesser 'I' is replaced by the understanding of the greater 'I' which sees, behind all the separate forms of the physical world, the one life, the one essence, and really *feels* that this expanded 'I', this new self, is an integral part of the one life permeating the whole universe. This is a tremendous expansion of understanding and must result in a complete change of attitude to one's fellow men.

In the last analysis, purity is largely a question of motive. If an action is triggered by a personality desire backed up by the use of the mind, it will be characterized by impurity. If, on the other hand, the impulse to action comes from the soul, or true essence, then the action will have the characteristic of purity, within the limitations resulting from the degree of control the soul has over the personality. Absolute purity can only exist when entire freedom from control has been brought about through the willing co-operation of the personality with the desires of the soul, and all necessity for control has evaporated.

What all this adds up to in practical terms is that the mind is being freed from the restraints that the personality imposes on it, and also from the obstructions that prevent the generation of its full power. Whereas before, it would have been dangerous to wield this power without the enlightenment that knowledge and the sincere practice of its compulsions brings, it is now safeguarded by the will that can direct it only for the good of mankind. First and foremost, we have to acquire a degree of mind control, and the habit of meditation. Then we have to study and absorb the new knowledge that will give us the understanding of our true situation.

These two preparations that have to be made before this tool can add to the energy that will flow down from the higher mind, must be carried out thoroughly and without impatience. They must be regarded as ends in themselves. One must, too, know at what one is aiming, and be conversant with, at least, the next step along the way. A sincere desire to direct all one's efforts for the good of one's fellow men must be behind all thought and all actions.

It will seem that sacrifices must be made, and these in prospect may appear unwelcome, unless one has clearly in mind the reward of service gladly performed, and feels deeply the unity of life that one is serving. The preparation of learning can come by reading, or by listening; it may take time for the mental digestion that is necessary for the intake of such new knowledge to serve up its findings to the conscious mind. Nothing should be accepted on the authority of any written or spoken word. One has to wait for the confirmation that will come from the inner being. This will be channelled down from the higher mind to the brain. One must have patience. The time necessary for this process depends on the extent to which the individual has already been introduced to the scenery of esoteric knowledge.

There may be an instant response, or it may, in some cases, take years for the full revelation of the new truth to take its place with the root assumptions on which he bases his idea of reality. Purely intellectual acceptance is not enough; you cannot argue yourself into acceptance; and a blindly believing reaction leads inevitably to fanaticism.

It must be left to the subconscious mind to cultivate the place where the new ideas can safely be rooted, either among friends, or in well weeded soil. This matter of learning is where so many go wrong, usually through being anxious to make use of the knowledge before it has become a deeply established part of one's basic assumptions of reality. In this function of sorting out what is to be accepted, the subconscious mind has immense critical faculties for sifting and selecting material to be served up to conscious thinking. However, learning only gives one a map of what lies ahead. The road must be travelled in physical reality. This is where the active clearing process comes in.

A further preparation is the important one of thinking and acting in one's daily life in conformity with the new knowledge. This will result in the gradual weakening of the position of the personality as a centre of reference for all thought and action, and developing a practical, outgoing love for one's fellow men, and the living creation in which we find ourselves. This, in contrast to the earlier preparation, requires outward rather than inward-looking attention.

Many reactions to events (including conversation and discussion), will tend to revert automatically to the old pattern. A policy of 'stop, think, readjust', will have to take the place of what was the natural reference to the 'I', the personality. This presupposes a constant recollection, because the new design for living will not replace the old until it has become a natural response, that is, until the 'will to love' is as great as the 'will to live'. Until this happens, the procedure will be: first recollect, then think and readjust, and only then reply or act as one's vision of the new reality demands.

This rather cumbersome routine will soon become irrelevant, as the natural response to all events is triggered by love and understanding instead of by the personality. It is in this way that the channel to the higher mind is being cleared for the power that

will then only be used wisely and safely for the benefit of
mankind. The obstruction of personality desires — or perhaps it
would be better to say the louder call of the personality — no
longer prevents the higher mind being heard by the lower mind
and the brain. It is not only that the voice of the higher mind
must be heard, but also that the purity of lower mind must be
such that it can convey accurately to the brain what the
higher mind has revealed. The power in an atomic reactor is not
available until the particular conditions are realized in which the
release of this power becomes possible. Mind-power, as we at
present experience it, is under the same kind of restriction so
that, until we produce the right conditions for its full release, it
cannot be forthcoming.

Purity, then, is the ultimate tool of quality that we gain access
to. All the tools that I have been writing about have to be used as
techniques, but then it is equally true that machine tools
necessitate an allied technique without which the tool cannot
function. With the mind, perhaps, the technique is more
apparent than the tool itself, and it is in the various techniques
that we fail so lamentably. We also do this very significantly in
the technique of living, which is clearly based on wrong assumptions. Our present power is quite adequate for these
assumptions; they will have to be lifted to the realm of the higher
mind as will also our technique of living, if we are to become the
kind of human beings that our real essence promises.

CHAPTER TWENTY-ONE
TIME:
A SETTING-UP TOOL

Time as a tool of the mind seems perhaps too obvious to find a place in a book which is dealing mainly with the development of new techniques of using the mind, or improving those already to some extent in use. But time is something about which many of us do not think clearly. There are usually two inaccuracies which we believe give us a satisfactory account of time as we experience it. These are, firstly, that time is what the clock gives us, and secondly, that time is something which exists in its own right. Neither of these statements is true.

We experience two kinds of time, clock-time and mind-time. Clock-time is purely arbitrary, a division of the earth's revolution on its axis into twenty-four equal periods, or the movement of some other heavenly body in relation to the earth. It is therefore a quality of something else. Mind-time, on the other hand, is given us by the continual sequence of mental states, the flow of thoughts through the mind. Periods of mind-time are therefore not equal. This is the time of our inner experience; it is a quality of our thinking. It is all the time we *know*. Clock-time we know *about*. We live by clock-time, or try to, because of its convenience in regulating our daily activities.

If one is deprived of all indications of diurnal change, meals at regular hours, and all the other matters that make, for us, the passing of clock-time, we become completely unable to discern what time of the day it is, or how long we have been isolated in this way. Time, for a person in such a situation, is measured by what is passing through his mind.

We do develop a sense of clock-time so that, during the normal actions of the day we can frequently, and with great accuracy, tell the duration of some activity, or even the time one has been waiting for something to happen. But this is rather like a person who has 'perfect pitch' and can always sing the note middle C on the piano. There is also a biological clock to which we become tuned subconsciously. It is this clock that enables us to awake from sleep and know quite accurately what the clock-time is, or to arrange for the subconscious to wake us up at a time decided on the night before. This is probably a calculation made from the regular beat of the heart, body-time perhaps. It is not made much use of.

The real time that we feel as passing or flowing is simply the result of a sequence of thoughts in the mind. If this statement is true, then one would conclude that, if all thinking stopped completely, the sense of time, of going on, would cease with it — and so it does. In states of deep meditation, when thought has first of all been controlled, then reduced to a pinpoint, and finally eliminated (which is the common aim of nearly all eastern meditations), there is no sense of time. There is nothing to produce the illusion of flow; there is no inner feeling of 'going on'. Maybe this is so, but of what use is this understanding of time, what practical help can it be to us who have to conduct our lives by clock-time? The answer to that, or perhaps a guide to the answer, is that while we order our lives by clock-time, we *think* in mind-time. And that is important.

Let us think for a moment about what happens in dream. We would expect dream-time to be exclusively mind-time. Much of it is, but we reproduce in our dreams the kind of events that happen during waking life, and we are constrained to let them happen as they do when we are awake, that is, in clock-time. But frequently the mind takes over control of the situation in its own impulsive way. For instance, we are going on a trip to the continent and have arrived at the ferry terminal. Suddenly without any apparent passage of time, we are driving off the ferry. Or, we may be dreaming of visiting friends in the USA. All of a sudden, we are there in their house talking to them. No bother of making a plane or boat reservation, none of the interminable queuing that air travel requires, just a wish and we are there. And that doesn't seem to be extraordinary. Of course it doesn't; mind-time is natural and it is 'home grown'. The mind is partly controlled by clock-time, when the dream follows the strict procedure of waking events, and partly by mind-time, when it is free of these shackles and the dreamer may be whatever, and wherever he thinks.

This state of affairs must give us some indication of what happens when we are out of the body, when we have discarded for good this particular physical form, and our mind is no longer limited by the restrictions it has imposed on us throughout our life. We then discover the amazing creative power of the mind (which, of course, we have had all along but didn't realize how real it was). We can go where we like; we can create whatever our mind is capable of. We don't have to learn manual skills to create say, a violin. Hey presto! and it's there, fully made at once. Dreams are frequently like this when we have escaped the habitual patterns of thought that have resulted from what is necessary in waking life. The state of deep meditation is not the same as that of a discarnate entity, because all thought has been eliminated and the mind has become aware on a higher plane where 'things' don't happen, where the mind is not concerned with events. It is the actual experiencing of the state of higher awareness that eliminates mind-time. A discarnate entity, who has recently left the physical body, is still aware, and will be for a period, of events in clock-time. He still remembers the activities of his physical life. Time will behave for him, therefore, much as it does in dream. Sometimes it will appear to follow the pattern of sequence that was the habit when in the body, and sometimes it will switch this sequence to what is going on in the mind. Gradually this latter state will take over as earth memories sink below the level of consciousness.

I said a little earlier that we order our lives by clock-time, but we *think* in mind-time. It is in thinking this difference out that we realize why time is a tool of the mind, as of course it should be. Mind-time, if the words mean anything, *must* be a tool of the mind. But it is a tool more in the sense of a technique than some of the other tools I have written about. Time, I make no apology for saying again, has no existence in its own right, so that it cannot be something that the mind *uses*. It is the way of using the mind, the sequence that thinking produces, that must be employed efficiently. It is this sequence that *is* time, and we must learn to eliminate all that interferes with it. What we intend to be the flow of our thoughts must be kept to the point. We have to learn to control the sequence; we are then learning to control time. This ability to control the sequence is what the previous chapters have been about.

We find that clock-time always tends to interfere with our thinking. We are sitting down to work on some problem when the thought crosses our mind that the joint for lunch should be put in the oven. That is clock-time interference. Or we are meditating early in the morning, and the thought intervenes that the allotted time must not be exceeded because a visitor is expected immediately after breakfast. We are so scheduled that something clock-time requires of us is never far from our mind. These continual living reminders have to be eliminated as we learn to remain in mind-time for our thinking. When we are concentrated on our thinking, the irregularity of mind-time compared to clock-time cannot worry us. But for our daily activities someone had to invent clock-time. This probably only happened as the day's occupations became more varied than they had been in the simple life of hunting, eating and sleeping.

Today, mind-time is affected by emotion, interest, sleep and other kinds of unconsciousness, by pain, anticipation, and many other occupational hazards. All these feelings either accelerate or decelerate the rate at which we feel time to be passing. It is only as we eliminate such disturbances that mind-time comes to order, but it does this only to eliminate itself! For the disturbances are the product of thinking, the reaction of the emotional body to various kinds of thought. All concrete thinking must have some result on this thing we call our personality, and this result inevitably constitutes a disturbance, slight or even imperceptible though it may be. So that it is concrete thinking itself that has to be stopped, and with it, of course, mind-time, the recorder of our thinking states. We have to be clear about this, for it is a simple fact; no thinking, no time.

This somewhat paradoxical conclusion means, of course, that when we are indulging in concrete thinking, we cannot entirely eliminate disturbances, but we can learn to limit and control them.

Mind-time, although it is the powerful originator of time, has its limitations in our present-day ambition to 'extend the frontiers of science'. It cannot, for instance, be used in mathematical calculations; it cannot be represented by symbols that have a constant meaning, because it is not itself constant. The mathematician uses time as any other natural phenomenon, such as weight or gravity, that can be calculated; but time itself cannot be measured, for there is nothing to measure it by. The time we use, and which the mathematician uses, clock-time, is measured by the regular (within acceptable limits) movement of some physical body, whether very large or very small (as in the modern quartz watch). But what can measure the movement of the body large or small that we have selected as our basis? If we struggle to deal with this problem, clock-time will become an infinite regression as we retreat further and further into the heavens to find bodies with which to measure the time of our standard.

It is the beginning of a true realization of the self when we understand that clock-time is not a thing of mystery as so many writers would proclaim it to be. It is certainly not a thing that we should give such prominence to in our daily lives, a prominence that, for most people is exalted into an existence in its own right. Time is a thing that flows? It isn't and it doesn't. In order to establish the right balance in our lives, we must realize that there is a time for clock-time and a time for mind-time. All deliberate concrete thinking and, much more importantly, all abstract thinking must be done in mind-time. To do this, the sequence of thought must be controlled and provided with the requisite energy. All the previous chapters have been describing the various ways in which this should be done. We have, first, to recognize mind-time, and then learn how to make use of it. This requires a very different attitude to that required for the use of clock-time. For clock-time we allocate priorities, so that the things we plan to do can be carried out in the clock-time available. When they can't, we cut our programme or alter our priorities. For mind-time, we have no priorities, we simply have an aim, the problem to be solved, the philosophical idea to be thought through. There is no question as to what comes after; we cannot give ourselves a clock-time limit, or rather, we should not do so. To use mind-time aright means bringing to bear all the available tools for the particular kind of thinking to be done, so that the sequence is strongly connected, purposeful, and free from disturbance of all kinds. That is what thinking should be, and what it can be.

I can understand that there may still be doubt in my readers' minds about my repeated statement that time has no existence in its own right. We can satisfy ourselves that, for us, time *is* the going-on that we sense from our thinking, from the continual succession of mental states. But what about the rest of the world? What about a flower or a rock? If these possess a time dimension, as is commonly accepted, where do they get it from? If it is true that time has no existence other than as the succession of thoughts in the mind, how can a rock be said to exist in time, which it obviously does? This is a difficulty that stems from our wrong understanding of time. It has been a convenient habit to put all phenomena into a 'frame' of time, and this has led us to believe that this 'frame' actually exists.

We have to start with the premise that we have a sense of time; that the real, live time we feel is the result of the way we think. It is very much the same kind of feeling as the sense of beauty that we get from a scene, an object, or a person. It is a construct of the mind. Now, if you feel that a rock cannot have its own primitive sense of going on, then you must give it existence in *your* time. That will obviously not be its whole existence, because it will certainly outlive you! You can, if you like, credit it with a time existence covering several or many thousands of peoples' lives. That is an attempt to explain time from your point of view. It is not rock-time. The rock only exists for you as part of your experience of time and what fills it. When that experience ceases then the rock, for you, ceases with it.

But the real answer to the problem of the rock needs a rather bolder step for the mind. Everything in this world, in the universe, is conscious. Some things we regard as living but not conscious — the vegetable world, for instance. Others we regard as inanimate or unconscious such as minerals, crystals, and everything that doesn't obviously exhibit signs of life. This is a view based on surface observation only. We know enough today to realise that it is not a true one. We know that the pulsating life of the atom exists in all those things we consider dead. Do we really want to believe that the atom is an automaton set spinning by some outside power, and without any directing purpose of its own? It would relieve this dead-end of thought to acknowledge that consciousness is there, primitive perhaps and difficult for us to imagine, but a consciousness that gives it existence, the power to attract and repel, and its own time, just as we have ours.

It is a much more comfortable and logical belief, that consciousness exists in a descending scale of scope and complexity from superhuman beings down through the human, animal, vegetable, to the mineral kingdoms. One consciousness expressing itself through vehicles which, in their varying degrees, limit the extent to which God-consciousness can be manifested. Each material object therefore, however inanimate it may appear to be, possesses its own inherent consciousness which, whatever else it does, must give it its time; not as we understand time as the sense of going on, certainly, but in some other less sophisticated more rock-like way, is time presented in this primitive consciousness.

This is, perhaps, the most difficult aspect of time for us to accept, because it steps outside the problem of time to that of the consciousness of matter. It has always been an uncomfortable partnership that has existed between the live and dead matter of the universe. The dead has never been to me very convincingly dead, and now with the scientist's view of the erstwhile dead matter, it is no longer a tenable differentiation. There is no such thing as dead matter. The thing we call time has its counterpart in every created thing in the universe, without distinction. The crystal chimes its hours, probably in a much more constant manner than our mind does ours. Somewhat higher up the scale of mind than the crystal, we have been able to elevate this particular quality of the working of our mind into what we call time.

CHAPTER TWENTY-TWO
'BEYOND MIND'

Some of my readers may feel that all that I have suggested that should be done to make thinking efficient is enough to prevent one doing any constructive thinking at all! Quite apart from the attention to the mechanics of thinking which will produce more effective results, there is probably a suspicion that these practices are leading somewhere else. And so they are.

The object of this book has been to bring out the extraordinary power that is inherent in the mind, and to stimulate more of it into action than we usually do. This may have raised a suspicion that mind is rather more than we understand it to be. In all the discussions in previous chapters, I have tried to put into practical terms what has to be done in order to bring the particular tool into action as effectively as possible. Most of these require the clutter that continually disturbs the mind to be eliminated, as far as this is possible. This has two important effects. Firstly, it enables the mind to put more energy into its thought, and secondly, it starts the process of making conscious contact between lower and higher mind. This is a very significant step, because it leads to the conscious awareness of the higher self, the thinker, the true essence, or soul. When this contact has become more than occasional flashes, there ensues a gradual takeover of the 'I' by the soul, that is, a take-over from the personality, which, at present, constitutes the 'I' for most of us.

These changes have their response in the business of practical living. This is an absolute necessity. There cannot be progress in the mind alone. That would lead inevitably to sterile theory-making and benefit no one. It must be followed by personality action in conformity with the new thought. If, for instance, one is convinced that humanity is of one source, and that brotherhood in this sense is a deeper relationship than that of physical kinship, then one's whole attitude to mankind must be based on this conviction.

The physical world is where all our theories are worked out. It is here that we have all the ingredients and opportunities for putting thought into action. It is in the world of personality contacts that we can generate relationships based on the love stemming from the knowledge that humanity *is* one family, that the phrase 'brothers under the skin' is a reality that we have to incorporate in our lives, and behave accordingly.

All esoteric work, and working on the mind as the chapters of this book propose, *is* esoteric work, has to find its fulfilment in the hurly-burly of everyday living. The full programme of the committed man consists of three basic elements, learning, meditation, and doing. Without meditation, learning cannot make the contact with higher mind that is necessary to convert it from cold intellectualism to a loving part of the 'I'. Without the doing, it cannot prepare the personality for the takeover by higher mind and soul, and eventually the entry in real practical living terms into the Kingdom of God. It is not just an intellectual exercise, or the gaining of more knowledge for the sake of increased power. It is the means of making that essential readjustment of values that will put material satisfactions into their proper relationship with spiritual insights. It is all the most practical of work, bringing a new light to everyday activities. It is no dreamer's recipe, but a programme for clear, concise thinking, and relentlessly monitored action.

It is mind that has the task of clearing away the dross of old crystallized thinking, and opening up the new channel of contact. It is mind that will hold us back if it remains at the beck and call of the personality. All progress towards the realization of our potential has to be made by mind. It is mind that holds within itself the seeds of our full promise as spiritual beings. Nothing holds us back from this high state but the control which the personality at present has over mind, holding it tied to the material satisfactions that give us the spice and variety of our living, and blinding us to the far greater joys that conscious contact with the higher self will bring.

What is required for the righting of our topsy-turvy sense of values is a programme of self-effort. Sitting at the feet of a guru and basking in the warmth of his spiritual aura won't do the work for us. The way has to be pointed out, certainly, but the directions should be brief, and the teaching must thereafter come from the inner self, until the seeker is ready for the next forward step. This self-teaching will come from that part of the mind that knows already, but has great difficulty in imparting its knowledge to the lower mind and the brain. The higher mind is there, we all have it, but it is masked by the constant occupation of the lower mind with the attractions of the material world and the pull of the senses. There is no time for listening to the messages from the higher mind, and there won't be until the seeker has learnt to still the incessant chatter in which the lower mind continually indulges, and to turn the direction of its attention from the outer kaleidoscope to the inner source of enlightenment, the still small voice that will be heard when the hubbub has subsided.

There is too much guru-hunting going on, in this country and in the west in general. In itself, that is an indication that mankind is beginning to look for the reality behind the effervescent surface that the present time displays. It is unfortunate that so many of these gurus like to amass a great following of disciples. Too much learning and too much listening has the result of encouraging the seeker after self-development to postpone the task of getting down to the work that he must do on himself. There is no alternative to learning, meditation, and doing; a little learning, regular meditation, and a lot of doing; and above all, the dogged persistence that doesn't expect quick results, but perseveres in the confidence that one is under way. Twists and turns in the road ahead will be revealed when the time comes, at present the intention must be to keep on keeping on.

One should not expect things to happen in a hurry. The channel to the higher mind has to be cleared by force, force of the kind that wears or clears away by constant repetition — the dripping tap, or the trickle of water drilling out a rock. That is the kind of mind-force that we have readily at our disposal at present, and it is sufficient to clear a path through the mass of junk and irrelevancies that are blocking our conscious contact with higher mind. Because of the lack of mind-power, persistence is necessary, and therefore patience.

Each forward step in mental awareness has to be matched by a complementary advance in action on the physical plane. That is why we are here, and why we return to physical life time and time again — to complete an unfinished job. Eventually we shall have learnt all the lessons that our physical presence on this earth can offer us. The lures of the physical senses will have lost their appeal, and the physical body itself will no longer be a necessary place of residence for the 'I', in order to progress along the path towards full spiritual realization. That is a state where the 'I' aligns itself completely with the higher mind or soul.

Before this distant event can happen, we will have to test all our new knowledge of ourselves, our fellow men and the function of our planet in the scheme of things, in the field of our daily activity. It is in the home, at work, and in relation to the international scene, that the new values must first learn to function. Esoteric training, which for us is the work of establishing contact with higher mind, is essentially a practical undertaking. It is always here and now, whatever one's contact with the outside world may be, that what is learnt in meditation and in reading has to be put into practice.

In practical terms this means that too much must not be attempted at one step; the mind is able to accept much more than the physically-based 'I' is able to work on. Theoretical knowledge is easier to acquire than the digested knowledge of first-hand experience. Be content with small advances like the wise child in the game of 'grandmother's steps'. We, in the west, have to learn to develop in our nature something of the patience, determination and long vision of our eastern brother. We have developed our intellectuality to such a point that it is submerging the other side of mind — the intuition — which should now be coming into expression. The control and monitoring of the mind is now the quality to be developed in order to allow access to the intuition. For the intuition comes from higher mind; it has nothing to do with the logical processes of the lower mind, except in its interpretation. It is already functioning spasmodically in many people, but mostly unrecognized.

In a sense, the physical body as a whole is a tool of the mind. It is, at present, the field of receptivity used to form the 'I' that we feel to be ourselves. As the new awareness of mind's higher content begins to control our thoughts and actions, the reactions resulting from the physical body's field of contact have to be relegated to a role of secondary importance. They will eventually become entirely automatic. We are, at this time, and I mean the whole human race, facing a drastic readjustment of our values from a materially centred outlook to a spiritually directed purpose, spiritually directed because originating from the higher mind. That is the reason for the great confusion that exists in the world, demonstrated by the revolt against external authority, while the internal authority which must replace it has not yet taken over.

Earlier in this chapter, I used the word 'love'. It is that quality which the Christ came to demonstrate, that will revolutionize human relations, the intimate, the passing, and the international. But it is not love as we understand the meaning of the word. This new quality is *not* an emotion, it is an attitude of mind completely free of the emotion which both drives and clouds thinking. It comes as the result of the inner recognition of the human race as a family of brothers. Even in the intimate ground of our close family relationships, we seldom display this true love, a love that gives without ever counting on a return. The sort of love a mother gives to her child, when it is entirely dependent on her, gradually changes as the child develops a mind of its own. It is this independence of mind which must be acknowledged as the right of every human being, even when he is rejecting the love he is being given. We see this rigidly opposed in dictatorships, whether of the right or left. True love has a greater influence on our thinking than any other quality. When we love, we start from a different base. Things like criticism, feelings of superiority, and all those minor emotional disturbances that we react to with irritation, become completely foreign to our instinctive response.

True love is, in no sense, an expression of sentimentality. It does not have to be called into action by outside individuals or events. It is already there, the attitude with which one waits to greet all eventualities. It is strong and unshakeable because it is not dependent on personality reactions; constant and predictable because it does not feed on an expected response of returned love. We are all too short of love at the present time. The world is, by and large, an unloving place. And it is only we who can change this. There will be, and there must be, if humanity is to be directed on to a sane path, millions of men and women who will work to achieve this change of relationship to their fellow men. It has started, but there is not yet enough leaven to influence the whole, or sufficient kindling to set the world ablaze with love. But it will come; the wind of love is rustling the branches, and every day more and more are joining the band of those who see what must be done.

This may make reassuring reading, but what can *we* do about it? How can each one of us contribute to this change of relationship that is so vital to our future? There used to be notices at unguarded level crossings which read 'Stop, Look, Listen.' We have to start by creating a 'watcher' so that we can do this. Each thought and action has to be monitored before it is let loose to have its effect for good or ill. When we begin this habit of sincerely watching what we think and do, most of our hasty, unthought-out actions will never take place, and our unkind critical or deliberately hurting thoughts will be dismissed before they are allowed to dictate action. It is the restraint in little matters which, in the end will prove more effective than grand gestures, and can lead to a greater degree of change in ground feelings. We need to restrain the ambition to become a leader in light all at once, a decision which may have slowly been born by some strong momentary emotion. It has to be taken slowly. This is not a question of dramatic leaps, but of small persistent steps that can be embarked on with confidence.

One's relationship to one's fellow men, considering the world at large, is, after all, forged in the confines of family, friends and workmates, and it is here that the change must start. It is not a good plan to start out by trying to change one's feelings for, say, the Chinese or the Vietnamese; that will merely accentuate their separateness. One has to start at the centre and spread outwards. Start with the intimate circle, where the rough tongue is too easily aroused, and gradually let all those outside this circle be drawn into its embrace.

That is how love can start, not by some grandiose plan to sacrifice one's life for the good of some starving third world people. There are some who can do this, and are suited by nature and profession for the task. But for most of us, a less dramatic picture is what we should present ourselves with. We should try to express less intolerance in action in response to daily trials, less of the hasty word, less criticism, less resentment, more understanding, more consideration, more sharing, and more giving. It is a question of 'less and more', two simple words that can change the world. Perhaps it is a good thing that sex is often divorced from love so widely in the western world; it will leave room for a new interpretation of the word 'love' that will give us a target to aim at.

I have written in various chapters about the necessity for intuitional knowledge, that is, soul knowledge or knowledge from the higher mind, to be interpreted by the rational concrete mind and thence passed to the brain for action on the physical scene. This means that the concrete mind, which is the part of the mind that we use in our daily activities, must have attained a degree of acuity and development that will enable it to handle this new thought coming from the intuitional sphere. Similarly, the brain must have available the capacity to receive and process this new kind of information on top of all its other duties, so that it does not remain just 'pie in the sky'. In this connection, I would like to paraphrase what has been written by the Tibetan in *White Magic*, one of the books 'received' by Alice Bailey and published by the Lucis Press.

'Before work on the mental plane is possible, that is, work of making contact with higher mind, it is important to have a developed mind, a well nurtured intelligence, and also to have achieved some degree of mind control. For mind is the main creative factor and the utilizer of the energies of the cosmos. The potency of mind is inconceivable. Is it possible dimly to sense a state of affairs in mental realms analogous to that now seen in the emotional? Can we picture the condition of the world when the intellect is as potent and as compelling as is the emotional nature at this time? The race is progressing into an era wherein men will function as minds; when intelligence will be stronger than desire, and when thought powers will be used for appeal and for the guidance of the world, as now physical and emotional means are employed. That is why we must now give more attention to the way in which we use thought and the purposes for which we use it.'

There must be, at this time, when the increase in mental awareness is taking place all around us, a large amount of spare capacity in the brain waiting for the time when it is needed. In this connection, there was recently a very interesting programme on TV entitled 'The Brain'. It related the cases of young people who were able to carry out their daily activities quite normally, and had been educated to high standards, while possessing only a small proportion of the brain that is accepted as normal. One particular young man who had a brain scan by chance, was found to have only 5% of the amount of brain tissue that is considered normal. He is a physically quite sound and bright young man who had just taken a mathematical degree. This remarkable discovery was found to be very exciting and challenging by the doctors and scientists who had been investigating these unexpected facts revealed by the brain scanner. There is, however, a fairly obvious explanation for this surprising discovery which nobody seems to have considered. We probably need only a very small proportion of the brain neurons that we possess in order to accommodate the size of brain that we require to carry out our present very limited functions of thinking and action. This might mean that our heads need to be no larger than a grapefruit and still be able to accommodate the size of brain we need. But we are, as I have already remarked, on the edge of a significant expansion of consciousness, which will take us from our present limited expression in the conscious and subconscious, into the superconscious mental activity initiated from the higher mind. This is quite obviously going on slowly but surely all over the world. If we did not already possess a head of the size we do have, and a brain with a large amount of spare capacity, we would have to wait thousands of years before the necessary physical development could have caught up with that of the mind. It seems obvious, therefore, that the urge towards the awareness of higher mind, which is not a blind urge, has made provision in time, so that the benefit of higher mind and the contact with soul that this makes possible, should not be delayed by a lack of response in the physical vehicle. It would seem to me that this is what this startling discovery of complete normality with a small fraction of the usual available neurons is telling us.

Of course, with the abundance of neurons that is the normal allocation, the sites in the brain for the various activities of thought and action would naturally be spread out to cover the whole area, but that is not to say that this is necessary, and it has now been shown that it is not. In centuries to come, the population of active neurons will increase considerably and the organization of the brain will, in consequence, have become more complicated. This surfeit of neurons may be partly the reason why it is so easy for our minds to encourage our brains to unnecessary action, the sort of fiddling activities to which we are so prone, and in general, the automatic and immediate reaction to mind chattering may be the result of this waiting and unused capacity. In fact, the neuron glut is a hindrance to the control of mind that we need for exploring its higher reaches. It is too easy for the idle mind to receive an impulse from the brain, and there is always mind-stuff available to react, without conscious willing, to the inconsequent chattering brought about by this brain/mind reaction. That is just a thought by the way; it is not meant to be a serious contribution to mind control or an excuse for the lack of it!

If, as I have stated, the object of learning the proper use of all these tools of the mind is to increase the power of mind and to bring into action areas of mind now beyond contact, and if one must expect a long period of striving before the activity of higher mind via lower mind to the brain can become a fact in our lives, then there is one important matter that I have only briefly touched on that should be discussed. That is the continuity of consciousness that is necessary for this to be possible.

Continuity is a straightforward word. We know about it not only as 'one damn thing after another', but also as the ability to wake up in the morning after being out of the conscious world, and continue with one's life as though there had been no break. The complete break that sleep brings about, and the obvious fact that consciousness must continue through it although it is not registering, should give us all the conviction we need to treat death in the same way.

For our continued mental and spiritual progress, continuity is essential. The lessons we have to learn in order to put our newfound knowledge into practice are found here on earth in abundance. We don't yet know whether they can exist elsewhere, but we do know that we leave this earth at death with an unfinished job. It is therefore a comfortable thought that, after an interlude, short or long depending on circumstances, we should return to the familiar earth to take up the thread of sorting out the personality and becoming acquainted with soul, from where we left off through our unavoidable departure.

I am not using the word reincarnation, partly because there is a good deal of misunderstanding about its precise meaning, and partly because continuity is a simple expression of something we already understand and accept. It cannot be in the mind of the modern intelligent, searching individual with a logical constructive belief, that this life is the only chance we get to learn the lessons required to develop our full spiritual maturity in an environment which seems eminently suitable in which to do this. We are not ready or worthy of heaven when we leave this earth, or very few of us are, and however wicked we may have been, we have not really earned hell in the short span of one human life. If one accepts continuity, and it is difficult for a thinking person not to, for he is unable to *think* himself out of existence, his body, yes, but not his thinking self, and if one believes that the job of self-education is not completed in one life, then a series of return visits to this earth is the inevitable conclusion.

There is, of course, a lot of evidence of those who remember their earlier lives, but much of this can be given another equally plausible explanation. The proof does not lie in such evidence; it lies within the soul-influenced mind of each individual. We are leaving the time when concrete proof is required for all statements of truth, or rather, we have included, under the term 'concrete', proofs that do not require the action and appearance of physical matter. But we have not yet accepted that what mind produces is as real as the most solid matter we know. There will come a time when mind-born certainty will be more valid for us than physically demonstrated fact, but we shall have to learn to discern when the truth being presented is coming from higher mind, and is not a construct of the logical lower mind and therefore liable to error. The case of continuity beyond death will be one of the truths that will come to us through higher mind experience. If, instead of looking to parapsychology or ESP for proof of this continuity, we work at developing the contact with soul, we shall find a sense of permanence that counts death as being an interlude between excursions to this earth. These repeated visits to 'classroom earth' can be seen as interludes, too, between the freedom of a different kind of existence unhampered by a physical body. When we understand that proof from inside is more valid than any outside demonstration, then we shall find the fact of continuity, which is firmly established through sleep, also being established beyond death, before that experience is again ours.

But, a willing listener may ask, if that is so, why don't we remember our previous existences? That in itself is not remarkable, for we don't remember all our dreams, in fact, some of us remember very few of them. The subconscious operates a mental barrier which limits its access to the conscious mind, and a very sensible precaution this is too, for the conscious mind has enough to deal with as it is, and we have little enough control over it. Thoughts from dreams would constantly interrupt our conscious thoughts and actions, and make it much more difficult to acquire even that degree of control that we have. The memories of previous lives lie deeper within the subconscious than our dreams, and therefore the mental barrier is denser and usually quite impenetrable. Apart from the interruptions to the normal working of the mind these could cause, they could also be potential initiators of repressions that would have serious results on the physical, emotional, and mental bodies. This does, of course, happen from time to time, when the memory of some event from a previous life manages to break through the curtain. There are some hypnotherapists who deal with such cases, and are able to regress a patient back to the event in the previous life, the memory of which is causing the trouble. We may well be influenced, to some extent, by memories that seep through the mental curtain, but with insufficient strength to do any damage. These we are able to deal with through the discriminatory action of our minds.

There is one great obstacle to this rational view of a continuity of consciousness which gives the human being a long succession of sojourns here on earth in which to work on his progress from animal to spiritual man. That obstacle is the sense of finality that death at this time presents to most of humanity. Our current conviction of temporality and fear of possible non-existence after death, is a natural result of equating our 'I' with the physical body. Most of us regard the essential 'I' as this physical body plus its mental and emotional associations. It is therefore natural that we should regard death as the end of all this, and since we have nothing to put in its place of which we are consciously aware, the fear of total extinction is very real. This state of uncertainty lies within our own power to remedy. We don't have to be polarized in our physical body; we know enough to realize that there is a more permanent essence that lies deeper than the skin and bones of our bodily structure, but we don't do much about it. We can, if we so wish, take steps to make contact with this deeper essence, and, whether you call it the soul of the Christian teaching, the pure mind of the Buddhist sutras, or give it any other name, it can become the foundation of the 'I' sense, replacing the physical body from that position. It stands to reason that we cannot be certain of continuity until we *feel* ourselves to be something other than the perishable body. We have to relate the 'I' to something that is not of the body, but we have to do this from experience, not from theory or in obedience to dogma.

This search for the essence of being requires a method and patient persistence, but humanity is now ready for the widening of mental awareness that this entails, and signs are abundant that many are already taking the first tentative steps. The method is, of course, meditation, but it has to be the right kind of meditation. So many systems that are now being introduced are not really suited to the particular temperament and mental level of the western individual. Further, they are not, for this age, aimed at the right target. The methods to be employed in spiritual training must change over the ages, and we are at present going through a time when the human race is ready for a great leap forward. This readiness makes it necessary for new, intensive training towards a particular end — that of making contact with man's true essence and gradually bringing the personality under its control. This is what our meditation should have in its sights. The steps to this realignment should be clearly indicated, so that each meditation form has its limited objective. This is putting meditation on an organized basis, in line with any other undertaking that we embark upon.

This undertaking is nothing less than a search within, a search to extend the mind in a direction which we do not normally follow, and a persistent effort to open up a connected line of thought from our logical, concrete, rational mind, to wherever we imagine the higher mind to reside. The limiting area of such a search has to be determined, and the creative imagination brought into use to represent the mental action in some pictorial form. This is essential, until such time as experience will reveal the substance of what is being achieved. The act of using the creative imagination will be replaced by the fact of experiencing the actual contact with higher mind, and learning how to deal with its message. In addition to this, there has to be a careful examination of the rubbish and cover-ups that have, up to now, been successfully hiding what is to be revealed from our understanding.

So much of our thinking on matters that relate to our true being has been conditioned by convention. We need to have not only an open mind, but also an adventurous one. There are guidelines, of course, and these can be had from many sources. At present, the soul or essence is being kept firmly in the background by the complete dominance of the personality, with its loud cries for attention from the senses, and its concern for the immediate comfort and wellbeing of the physical, emotional and mental combine.

The difficulty in the search we have to make, is that we do not know exactly what it is we are searching for. The guided and confident use of the creative imagination is vital to success. Each individual must determine how to visualize this essence in his meditations. A generally accepted form is of light, which is indeed the way in which we shall be conscious of it. There is nothing mystical or airy-fairy about this attempt to forge a channel to higher mind. It is a down-to-earth practical undertaking with a clear objective in view. It *is* esoteric, because it is concerned with the energy that constitutes the essence, but all who wish to follow the esoteric path must learn to be pragmatic, however difficult this seems when working in mental matter.

In the decades to come, we are going to have to learn to turn our attention, which is now riveted almost exclusively on the things we can see, to the things we can't see. Further than that, we must learn how to build our reality from this new class of contacts, instead of from those of the coarse physical world. We shall discover that what we now consider as reality is very largely composed of the end products of what stands behind, that all creation is the result of energies of which we can become aware, some of which we shall even be able to see with our physical eyes. This is surely an exciting prospect, that a completely new world of experience will open up to us, and that it will transform the kind of life we lead from one of a closed self-interest, to one of living out a true sense of brotherhood. It will be a life where the evil emotions of today, of hate, greed, and power-seeking of all kinds, both in the close circle of our daily activities and in the wider international scene, will be eliminated. They will disappear, not by regulation, but through education, the learning of the true situation of the human family. All this will come from the belief that there is something in the mind that is higher and more rewarding than what we now know, and the incentive to start the simple process of advancing into this new territory by the aid of the creative imagination.

There is little more to be said. We know where we stand; we have the tools, and the intelligence to learn how to use them.

INDEX

MIND YOUR BODY
A PRACTICAL METHOD OF SELF-HEALING

E. H. Shattock. Explains a remarkable visualization technique employed by author to heal his arthritic hip joint and reduce his enlarged prostate, after studying the physiology and pathology of the affected areas. This is not a revelation of some psychic ability; it isn't any kind of faith healing, neither is it an example of mind over matter. It is quite simply what one might call 'body engineering', but of a special kind. Effectiveness of this self-treatment depends on the accuracy of visualization and the degree of concentration with which it is held — and lots of patience.

A MANUAL OF SELF-HEALING
USING MENTAL ENERGY FOR OVERCOMING COMMON AILMENTS

E. H. Shattock. Energy follows thought! This remarkable book shows how to instruct the automatic mind — the part of the subconscious controlling 'automatic' actions — to initiate healing procedures for broken bones, 'frozen shoulder', sore throats, infected teeth, arthritic joints, polyps, etc. Author used this method successfully in treating his enlarged prostate gland and his arthritic hip. The techniques employed train the mind through three essential functions; focus (or concentration), mind-picturing, and breathing. Using these techniques, a body could be instructed not to reject a heart or kidney transplant, eventually obviating the need for continuous drugging.